Drama as Education

*an argument for placing drama
at the centre of the curriculum*

Gavin M. Bolton
University of Durham, England

Longman

Longman Group Limited
Longman House
Burnt Mill, Harlow, Essex CM20 2JE, England
and associated companies throughout the world

First published 1984
ISBN 0 582 36198 2

Set in 11/13pt Ehrhardt, Linotron 202

Printed in Singapore by
Huntsmen Offset Printing (Pte) Ltd

Contents

1 The first part of the twentieth century   1
2 The middle of the twentieth century –
   Peter Slade and the Speech and
   Drama experts   22
3 The 1960s and 1970s – Brian Way and
   Dorothy Heathcote   42
4 Community theatre and other
   influences on drama in school   60
5 The 'game' of drama   76
6 Emotion and the game of drama   105
7 Drama as experience – aesthetic and
   educational   140
8 In context   165

Bibliography   189

Index   201

Acknowledgements

One day someone will write a complete history of drama in education and will turn, as I have, with gratitude for information and inspiration to the researches of Tim Cox, John Deverall, Mike Fleming, David Griffiths and Ken Robinson.

I am indebted to Durham University for giving me sabbatical leave in order to write the book and for the generous grant it gave me towards my travel to schools both in England and in America.

I would like to thank my wife for her patience and understanding (and endless cups of coffee!) during the six months of work and to my colleague, Barrie Wetton for taking on so many of my teaching commitments in my absence. Many thanks, too, to Kathy Gordon, a truly professional secretary and manuscript typist.

We are grateful to the following for permission to reproduce copyright material:

Calouste Gulbenkian Foundation for an extract from pp 44/5 *The Arts in Schools: Principles, practice and provision*, Calouste Gulbenkian Foundation 1982; Hodder & Stoughton Educational for extracts from *Child Drama* by P. Slade, 1954; the authors, Cecily O'Neil and Alan Lambert for extracts from their *Drama Structures*, pub. Hutchinson, 1982.

This book is dedicated to Dorothy Heathcote, educator, artist and friend.

In everyday life, 'if' is a fiction, in the theatre 'if' is an experiment.
In everyday life, 'if' is an evasion, in the theatre 'if' is the truth.

Peter Brook

1 The first part of the twentieth century

I am beginning this book with an historical account for two reasons. I hope it will go some way towards explaining to drama teachers and educational administrators why the drama 'scene' in schools might at times seem pointless, complex, contradictory or even trendy. All historical summaries are over-simplifications, but the risk of distortion is worth taking in order to cater for my second, more important reason which is critical to the theme of the book. In so far as this publication attempts to present a new thesis on drama education, it will be seen that in certain respects I want to turn the clock back, not with a reactionary intent, but in order to re-value some aspects of drama that have in recent years been neglected. It will be seen that the history of the subject has been fraught with rivalry, polarity and 'joining camps'. I want to look beyond these divisions to the nature of dramatic activity itself and to note how, in order to promote a philosophical ideal, rival pioneers have often only taken selective aspects of the activity in order to reinforce a case. I wish to rectify the balance by taking a broader view and by introducing a theoretical framework through which an eclectic view might be sustained.

I shall in the main confine myself to events in Great Britain, although I am well aware that the history of drama in other countries is not dissimilar. The influence that pioneers in this country have had and still are having on the Western world is fairly considerable. Many English drama specialists who emigrated to Canada and Australia in particular during the post-war years are to be found in teacher-training and university posts in those countries. Scandinavian countries have drawn on British sources for a flow of guest lecturers over a number of years as has

1

South Africa, especially since its South African Drama and Youth Theatre organisation became genuinely multi-racial. People such as Maisie Cobby, Peter Slade, Brian Way, John Allen, John Hodgson and Dorothy Heathcote have travelled world-wide, and Brian Way's publication *Development through Drama* (1967) has been translated perhaps more extensively than any other educational drama literature, so that, for instance the Japanese are currently showing a great deal of interest in his work.

Because it will be necessary to be critical of principles and methods which these and other exponents have advocated, let me say at once that such criticism is offered out of a deep respect for their work. For instance, I had the privilege of being trained in my early teaching days by both Peter Slade and Brian Way, two remarkable men who dedicated their professional lives to creating a climate of understanding so that teachers might feel free to trust the natural dramatic expression of each child. It is difficult for young teachers today to understand just how innovatory such a philosophy was in the 1940s, '50s and '60s. We now tend to take for granted those very values for which these two men spoke up with lone voices. But no interpretation of values, no principles or methods are sacrosanct. Slade and Way took us an astonishing distance on a journey, but we must not imagine, and they would not want us so to assume, that we had arrived. It is important that if this book succeeds in moving us even further along, the next decade of teachers throw out yet another challenge so that this publication is seen for what it is, yet another stage on the journey. Apart from Professor Coggin's (1956) attempt to give an historical account from Greek times to present day of theatre as a pedagogical instrument, the only evidence I have come across of scholarship in this field as it relates to this century is from three unpublished theses on which I have relied heavily for my sources by Tim Cox (1970), John Deverall (1979) and Ken Robinson (1981), and the most readable account given in the early chapters of John Allen's book, *Drama in Schools: Its Theory and Practice* (1979). The first of these

2

is particularly useful for the detail with which it documents the development of drama in education from 1902 to 1944.

Twentieth-century views of education

Two contrary views of education have been in continual conflict throughout this century. The traditionalist view has regarded the purpose of education as the transmission of knowledge. (This differs considerably of course from the American 'traditional' view which lays emphasis on behavioural modification). By 'knowledge', advocates of this philosophy have meant knowledge of a static impersonal kind, that which a culture can pass on from one generation to the next, that which a teacher refers to as facts or skills. It is knowledge of the kind which can be expressed in propositional terms: 'it is the case that . . .'. It is often referred to as 'knowledge that . . .' and the learning of skills as 'knowledge how . . .'. The metaphor that perhaps best meets this view of education is the 'empty pitcher' image, where something external to the child, valued by the teacher, is 'poured in' to the passive open-mouthed vessel, the teacher of course doing the pouring, and through the examination system, testing subsequent content of the pitcher and, indeed, through intelligence testing and the like, measuring its capacity.

The contrary assumption about education stems from the Romantic emphasis on the uniqueness, the importance and sacredness of the individual. The child, according to Rousseau, should 'be held in reverence', and be allowed to grow naturally and, by definition, in goodness. He writes in *Emile*:

> Let us lay it down as an incontrovertible rule that the first impulses of nature are always right; there is no original sin in the human heart (p. 56).

The teacher is to encourage this natural growth and protect the child from interference from the wicked adult world.

Respect for the child should predominate over any external knowledge. The appropriate metaphor taken from Froebel (1887) is that of a seed tended by a caring gardener, the teacher, who must patiently wait for the blossom that was always within it.

It seems unlikely that any extreme versions of these competing educational philosophies were ever put into practice. Perhaps A. S. Neill's (1964) Summerhill, more than any other institution, represented an attempt to move away from knowledge-centred to child-centred education, a revolution which John Dewey (1921) described in the following terms:

> The old education may be summed up by stating that the centre of gravity is outside the child. It is in the teacher, the textbook, anywhere and everywhere you please except in the immediate instincts and activities of the child himself . . . Now the change which is coming into our education is shifting the centre of gravity . . . The child becomes the sun about which the appliances of education revolve; he is the centre about which they are organised (p. 35).

One of the curious features many such 'progressive' writers on education shared was either a huge optimism that the 'revolution' was indeed about to take place or an unfounded conviction that it had actually done so. As Ken Robinson (1981) has pointed out, drama too had its share of optimists. Vail Motter as early as 1929 was writing of drama 'receiving increasingly widespread recognition' and nine years later Boas and Hayden (1938) were confidently reporting on drama work in schools as 'established practice'. The truth is that in spite of strong leads by educationalists and supportive reports by Government committees (Newsom, 1963 and Plowden, 1967), child-centred education has never gained control in this country. The writers of the so-called *Black Papers* (1969) have been venting their spleen on a very small proportion of our educational institutions, for in this continual conflict between two philosophies throughout this century, the

4

traditional 'empty pitcher' model tends to win in the end.

Explanations of why this is so go deep into our Western way of looking at the world. Scientific empiricism has discredited personal experience. Only that which can be verified by observation can be important. Neutrality and unanimity are the guardians of truth. As Marthinus Versfeld (1972) has put it: 'Descartes made the world safe for *thing*-thinking when he reduced the person to the epistemological subject' (my italics). And he continues:

> The kind of agreement and the kind of language which knowledge of things requires demands a sort of inter-change-ability among the investigators. To reach agreement they must be objective, they must be impersonal. They must lend their voices entirely to the thing, taken in abstraction from its existential individuation (p. 22).

Marthinus is making the point that whatever 'thing' is being looked at, it cannot be looked at for itself, but only as a specimen, and the observers cannot be important in themselves: just as the 'thing' has immediately to be classified, so they, the observers, have to operate as classifiers. Thus in our educational system we give prior status to facts and to the knowers of facts.

Introduction to the pioneers of drama in schools

I do not propose to give an account of the work of the great names in drama education. One day someone may take up that important task. I merely intend, in selecting a few of them, to examine their writings in so far as they reflect the writers' assumptions about such concepts as child-centredness, self-expression, the nature of knowledge, the function of the teacher, the nature of acting and drama as art. For these concepts will be critical to the thesis I shall present throughout this book. What follows in this chapter, therefore, is an attempt to identify philosophical trends, trends which, at the time of their emergence, were often too embedded in counter-ideologies, in

5

inner convictions and in the methodologies and practices of the pioneers to be made explicit. In looking at hidden assumptions in past practice we may better understand what we are doing or perhaps should be doing today. Far from rejecting out of hand earlier drama work as old-fashioned, it may be that if drama is to be at the centre of the curriculum, we need to find a new respect for what has been seen as traditional. But there must also be some rejection, not for reasons of trendiness or cults or expediency, but because after a century of drama in education we are better informed. Whereas our predecessors had intuitions about what was right, we must now attempt to look squarely at the concepts that underpin our practice. Our responsibility must be to find a rationale that can be understood by drama and non-drama teachers alike.

It might be expected that of the concepts listed above, child-centredness and self-expression could be the hallmarks of drama teaching. Certainly for all their differences in methodology, child-centredness does appear to be a feature to which all the pioneers have paid allegiance. We shall discover, however, that even for the most 'romantic' drama pioneers, the centre of gravity has never consistently rested in the child. Before moving on to look at individual pioneers, I need to elaborate upon a paradox, an ironical twist to our conception of drama which hinges on these two notions of child-centredness and self-expression.

Most drama educationalists have claimed that their work is child-centred, that what they are interested in is self-expression of each individual and indeed some have gone a long way to implementing such a philosophy. I shall try to demonstrate that the notion of child-centredness in drama has been a myth, that there has always been, to employ the same metaphor, an alternative pull of gravity to which even the most ardent advocate of self-expression, Peter Slade, has responded. I shall further argue not that they were wrong to give in to the 'alternative' pull, far from it, but that in over-stating the case for child-centredness they have often inadvertently misled their followers into believing that pure undisciplined self-expression should be the basis for dramatic education. The result has been that some teachers have either seriously encouraged the most uninhibited forms of free-expression (fortunately such teachers have been rare) or, more commonly, they have in practice shifted the centre of gravity away from the child whilst giving lip-service to self-expression. Much teacher training in drama has been based on this kind of self-deception.

It is not the case that drama teachers are given to an unusual degree of hypocrisy. In some ways the distortion has been, as we shall see, thrust upon them. For dramatic activity from when it was first introduced into our classrooms at the turn of the century was seen by some educationalists who were carrying the banner of the 'New Education' movement, to fit rather neatly with that movement's ideals. It seemed to epitomise child-centredness to an extent which drove Mr. Edmond Holmes (1911), a Ministry Inspector and leading figure in progressive education, in his Utopian view of education to recommend:

> In Utopia acting is a vital part of the school life of every class, and every subject that admits of dramatic treatment is systematically dramatised (p. 174).

But this recommendation has to be understood in the context of Holmes' philosophy which saw the function of education as fostering 'the child's whole nature, in other words, his soul' (p. 48).

Thus drama was becoming associated in some people's minds not just with any kind of self-expression, but with expression of the deepest kind. Drama pioneers at the beginning of the century did not invent child-centredness; a few articulate people were eager to endow drama with those special characteristics they wanted the New Education movement to stand for.

But child-centredness and self-expression were not the only catch-words of the New Education movement with which drama was to become associated. 'Learning by doing', 'activity method' and 'play-way' were to become absorbed into the drama teacher's vocabulary. The New Education movement that started in the 1870s, although taking many different forms detectable in distinct subsidiary movements, nevertheless collectively represented a reaction to the instrumental view of education. The glorification of the three Rs, reinforced by the 'payment by results' control over teachers' salaries, had led to a rigid form of rote learning that surely epitomised the 'empty pitcher' model of teaching. R. H. Quick (1902) described the reaction in the following terms:

> The New Education treats the human being not so much as a learner but as a doer and creator. The educator no longer fixes his eye on the object – the knowledge, but on the subject – the being to be educated. The success of the education is not determined by what the educated know, but by what they do and what they are (p. 525).

Perhaps more significant even than reaction to knowledge as facts to be remembered and recited was a change in our perception of a child. Evolutionists replaced the traditional view of children as 'little adults' with developmental theories to do with natural stages of growth. Indeed some pioneers of drama in school, Joseph Lee (1915) and Peter Slade (1954), were keen to identify natural stages in dramatic development, a view of the subject which has been theoretically sustained by Richard Courtney (1971) in Canada. Many Canadians today refer to·it as 'Developmental drama'.

The puritan view of play as a regrettable indulgence by children was also being challenged. 'He who plays as a child will play as a man,' John Wesley had warned. But evolutionists were taking an interest in child play activities and explanations were offered as varied and perhaps contradictory as 'recapitulation (Hall, 1904), 'pre-practice' (Groos, 1899) and 'repressed emotions' (Freud, 1952). Groos' view that a child learns to become an adult by *actively* trying out adult behaviour opened the door to considering the potency of activity as a means of learning.

The notion of 'activity method' crept into our classrooms at the beginning of the century. It is not surprising that such a concept seemed ripe for drama. 'Learning by doing' became the Progressivists' educational catchphrase, to be echoed throughout this century by the drama teacher's version of it: 'Drama *is* doing'. And, of course, an assumption shared by many educationalists and drama teachers has been that activity and child-centredness are inseparable bedfellows. It took the American educator John Dewey to convince progressivists that 'activity' in the classroom should have some purpose and that the child's environment was still a key factor in the child's learning. The centre of gravity was not to rest so much with the child as with his engagement with the world he lived in. But Dewey's message was slow in getting through to this country and a climate was created here in the early decades of this century that had the kind of curious effect referred to above on the way drama came to be viewed. Because it appeared to be pre-eminently an activity and (so it was supposed) properly child-centred, progressive educationalists such as Holmes gave tacit support to the notion that whatever was done in drama was right. Whereas the other arts might be examined critically, drama of all kinds and of varying standards was to be tolerated and indeed welcomed. Such implied views pleased neither non-progressive teachers nor drama teachers with a strong sense of standards in performance. The result has been that traditional teachers have viewed (and still view) drama with suspicion and theatre-minded specialists have found themselves constantly defending standards. Even today vast numbers of schools have no drama at all. This is due in part to a legacy of preciousness that the subject has inherited.

This then is the cruel irony of drama in education's history that will be illustrated more sharply when we look closely at the work of individual pioneers: that drama is not purely a child-centred activity in practice and yet its theorists write as if it is and, further, that in giving the impression to others that it is unerringly child-centred

9

drama teachers have unwittingly nearly brought about its demise.

The reader who believes that drama has been well-established in English schools may be shocked, but the fact is that drama has never been established in any permanent way in our system. One only has to glance at Connie and Harold Rosen's book, *Language of Primary School Children*, published in the early 1970s when, following Plowden's stamp of approval, progressive education in England was at its peak – just before the 'back-to-basics' battle-cry. They head their chapter on drama as 'In Search of Drama: More Questions Than Answers', and their opening paragraphs read as follows:

> Look for teachers who are interested in language work and you will have no difficulty in finding them. There is something to learn from their insights, imagination and sheer practical 'know-how'. But mention drama and they nearly always waver and seem unsure of their direction, or they will refer you to the school 'expert', something they would never dream of doing if we were talking about children's writing or reading. I share much of their uncertainty, and I cannot say that my visits to schools really resolved it. All the same, I think it would be helpful if others trod the maze with me, shared in my attempt to phrase the questions and began to discuss whether they agreed with my first tentative conclusions.
>
> Very little drama work goes on in primary schools. My own sample showed very little and this impression was confirmed by advisory staffs and drama specialists. I became more and more interested in the possibilities as I collected less and less (p. 196).

As I suggested at the beginning of this chapter, traditional views of knowledge are bound to take priority in this scientific, technological century. The paradox is that had drama pioneers been able to demonstrate that drama is concerned with *knowing* rather than with self-expression, the traditonalists might have been more ready to listen. But this is of course to ask the impossible, for as I have earlier asserted, drama was welcomed by progressivists *because* it appeared to be about self-expression – and drama teachers had to make sure it lived up to that myth.

Early pioneers

I do not suppose that many people today are even aware of a book written on dramatic method during the first decade of this century by Miss Harriet Finlay-Johnson, a village school head-mistress. And yet it is the only published example we have to date in which a teacher gives a full account of an integrated dramatic curriculum. (We have, of course, A. R. Stone's (1949) movement-based curriculum from the 1940s, and Joan Haggerty's vivid record of her Primary School experience was to follow in 1966, but she was brought into the school as a Drama specialist). Everything to be taught (History, Geography, Scripture, Nature-Study, Poetry, Shakespeare and Arithmetic) was adapted to dramatic action. Miss Finlay-Johnson's publication is intended to be a description of a teaching experience not a theoretical statement, but there are within its pages some extraordinary insights which at the time must have been quite revolutionary. I will merely list some of them: she believes in the child's natural dramatic instinct; she sees the process of dramatising to be more important than the product; she values both improvised and scripted work; she thinks an audience is irrelevant and discourages 'acting for display'; she lets children take initiative in structuring their own drama; she sees children's happiness as a priority.

One might have expected that such a teacher was working in the second half of this century rather than at the beginning. Indeed, had people taken more notice of her work, Peter Slade would not have had to fight such a battle in the 1940s and '50s. I remember as a young teacher in the 1950s under Peter Slade's influence, welcoming the idea of drama without an audience as if it were a new concept. Her work anticipated many such 'progressive' views. My purpose here, however, is to look more closely at what surely appears to be child-centredness.

Although in the long term Harriet Finlay-Johnson sees the value of such an approach as almost a spiritual preparation for adult life ('Am I quite wrong,' she asks, 'when I say that childhood should be a time for absorbing big stores of sunshine for possible future dark times?'), there is for her an academic objective in the short term which she takes for granted and which undoubtedly qualifies the child-centredness of her work: there is always a distinct body of knowledge to be learnt, a selection of historical or geographical facts on which the children can be tested. She is too enlightened a teacher to see this acquisition of facts as mere rote-learning in disguise:

> It may not be the facts themselves which are so valuable. It is the habit of mind formed while learning them which makes their worth (p. 97).

This smacks a little of the 'Latin is good for you' view of education, but at its best it suggests an interest in creating the habit of looking beyond the facts, to their implications. Perhaps this is to interpret her too generously but my reason for wanting to do so is to place her as the one notable fore-runner to Dorothy Heathcote. This will need much more explanation which will come later. For now let it suffice to underline the point that in the work of Harriet Finlay-Johnson we have a conception of drama that attaches considerable importance to subject-matter. The drama is used as a means of mastering content. Thus in a strange way this child-centred approach served the traditional requirements of education as transmitter of knowledge. Subsequently, many teachers must have adopted this dramatic method, but interestingly, no pioneer until Dorothy Heathcote has given it prominence. It has been a good example of the centre of gravity resting not with the child (in spite of appearances to the contrary) but with the child's *engagement* with his culture – or rather, the adult's culture.

An excerpt from one of Miss Finlay-Johnson's playlets (it is not clear whether the script is hers or her pupils) will indicate to the reader what she meant, for example, by drama illuminating history:

Enter two market women with baskets of wares. Apprentices cry, 'What d'ye lack?'

FIRST MARKET WOMAN Hast heard the news that Phillip hath sent a large fleet of ships to England against us?

SECOND MARKET WOMAN Odds, woman! thou dost surprise me.

FIRST MARKET WOMAN There are hundreds and hundreds of them, and I did hear that a man named Drake and some of his friends were playing at bowls down at Plymouth Hoe, when another man come riding up to them and told them that the Spanish were in the Channel. The good Queen, God bless Her! went down to see the army, riding on her grey pony.

Enter third market woman, while a man draws near to listen, eating a large apple.

THIRD MARKET WOMAN Do you know that the English are sending out fire-ships?

SECOND MARKET WOMAN Lawk-a-mussy-me! What are they?

THIRD MARKET WOMAN Why they are old vessels filled with tar, and gun-powder, and things that will burn easily. They turn these adrift among the enemy's ships and they either set fire to the other ships or blow them up.

SECOND MARKET WOMAN They say the Spanish ships sail in a half-moon shape?

MAN WITH APPLE Ah, it wants stout English hearts like mine to fight they Spaniards!

FIRST MARKET WOMAN Methinks your stomach is greater than your heart.

SECOND MARKET WOMAN Yes, judging by the size of his apple – but hark! here comes the Queen. We must be off to our stalls.

Enter Queen Elizabeth, Court Ladies and Courtiers.

In Caldwell Cook (1917) we have another 'child-centred' progressivist, who at the Perse School as a young English Master under the sympathetic eye of the headmaster, Dr. Rouse, demonstrated, somewhat to the distaste of his fellow public-school colleagues, that Shakespearian plays were not for studying but for acting. Innovatory as this seems to have been, he would not have been regarded as a key figure among the pioneers of drama education had it not been for his much wider vision of education. Indeed, his name has been to the fore in most recent attempts, however brief, by educationalists at historical surveys of drama in education. It is interesting that Richard Courtney (1968) in his introduction to a theoretical rationale, chooses to include Caldwell Cook in his account of major contributors, but not Dorothy Heathcote.

Cook's philosophy, as I have suggested, extended beyond a view of dramatic literature to a conception of play activity as a basis of education. He affirms, 'Play is one of the fundamentals of life, capable of anything but a further explanation' (p. 8). One might be misled into assuming that he is concerned with free expression, that here is an English master who was encouraging, for example, the 'creative writing' so popular in our schools in the post-war years. Far from it. In Caldwell Cook's work we have another instance of an alternative pull of gravity – this time towards strict artistic form. This is the key to understanding his teaching. He challenged his pupils to appreciate the craftsmanship of Shakespeare and other classicists and to aim at 'literary workmanship' in everything they created.

English was not a subject, not a method – it was an experience. Christopher Parry (1972), a former pupil of the Perse School long after Cook's retirement, still benefited from the school's dramatic tradition. He writes, 'For us English meant, chiefly, a happening in which we were all involved' (p. 3). Lucky Christopher Parry! Lucky Perse School! How many pupils today I wonder can speak of English in terms of experiencing it? Generations of

English teachers have missed their chance to emulate this teaching method. English in schools could have been given the distinctive status held by Physical Education (status, that is, as it is understood by the pupils themselves, not by pseudo-academics who disown anything not examinable), for Physical Education has managed to rise above a body of facts and principles to be studied; it has never been a method of teaching something else. And although it is neither of these, no-one would suggest it be withdrawn from the curriculum. For it has always been a worthwhile activity in itself where skills can be acquired as maturity and practice allow. This is what Caldwell Cook was doing for English.

Now what effect has this had on drama? Curiously, very little, for Cook was not teaching drama as drama. He was using a dramatic method so that his pupils could experience and enjoy English literature. This differs markedly in intention from Harriet Finlay-Johnson. For Cook there was not a tangible body of knowledge other than the craftsmanship of the artist. Thus for Cook the *content* of the drama was not an immediate objective; it was a means to an end. He did not use the dramatic mode as Harriet Finlay-Johnson does in the extract above to illuminate the facts of history, nor did he concern himself, as we shall see later Dorothy Heathcote might, with some particular inner meaning of a scene of a Shakespearian play to which he wanted his pupils to gain access through the medium of performance.

There is an assumption, though not stated by Cook in these terms, that if the pupils' attention is on the techniques required to portray the dramatic event, then by a process of osmosis, they are put in touch with the poetry of the plays. Something of this is reflected in the work of another pioneer, Joan Gilpin (1920) who, as headmistress of a private preparatory school, attempted to make the performance of plays the core of the school work. One of her ex-pupils commented, 'In *The Ancient Mariner* we plumbed depths of experience which are not within the

supposed range of children of 12 and 13.' Now this notion
that through the arts we can 'plumb depths' is something
that teachers either take for granted, ignore or actively
take a hand in. Chris Parry, writing in the early 1970s,
quotes from Josef Conrad's preface to *Nigger of the
Narcissus*: Conrad is writing of the purpose of the artist,
but Parry claims that the same eloquence should be applied
to what the English teacher is striving for. He should speak:

> . . . to our capacity for delight and wonder, to the sense
> of mystery surrounding our lives; to our sense of pity,
> and beauty, and pain; to the latent feeling of fellowship
> with all creation – and to the subtle but invincible
> conviction of solidarity that knits together the loneliness
> of innumerable hearts, to the solidarity in dreams, in
> joy, in sorrow, in aspirations, in illusions, in hope, in
> fear, which binds men to each other, which binds
> together all humanity – the dead to the living and the
> living to the unborn.

Parry is a teacher of English seeking to give spiritual status
to his subject, but most of his contemporary writers on
drama in education, for instance, John Fines and Ray
Verrier (1974), Chris Day (1975), Lynn McGregor (1976),
Cecily O'Neill et al. (1976), Peter Chilver (1978) and much
of my own writing (1979) were emphasising the social,
problem-solving characteristics of the subject. They have
been part of a trend that has chosen to ignore 'plumbing
the depths' in an aesthetic or spiritual sense.

Now Caldwell Cook did not ignore the possibilities; he
took them for granted. That the 'play-way' to education
was very much part of a spiritual and moral education was
in keeping with a tradition, started in modern times by
Friedrich Schiller (1795) and continued in Cook's life-
time by Herbert Read (1943), that linked play with art
and both of them with the highest form of education. But
Cook allowed the aesthetic experience to speak for itself.
This revealed itself in two ways. One was that he made
no attempt to structure experiences with poetic meanings
in mind, nor did he attempt to train the boys in the skills

of acting. The boys' responsibility was to show the play's action, *to make the events clear to an audience.* I am emphasising this view of performance for we shall see later that performing became something rather different from a presentation of a play's events.

If we see Harriet Finlay-Johnson and Caldwell Cook as innovators who in their different ways influenced progressive teachers during the early decades, the former introducing a dramatic method of teaching other subjects, the latter revolutionising the teaching of English, who do we acknowledge as the instigator of yet a third strand to the development of our drama in our schools during the same period? I am referring to 'speech-training', or 'elocution' as it was called in the early days, which began imperceptibly at the beginning of the century and gathered considerable momentum during the 1920s, '30s and '40s. There was no outstanding school-based innovator who was doing remarkable work with children. Rather the influence seemed to come from various committees and associations.

Tim Cox (1970) has pointed out that the first *Handbook of Suggestions for the Consideration of Teachers and others concerned in the Work of Public Elementary Schools* (1905) – to give it its full portentous title! – acknowledged that drama could be employed as a method in practising speech with infants, although even in this publication, Cox comments, an ambivalent attitude can be detected. He quotes from the *Handbook* its warning about dramatisation when reading aloud in class: '. . . exaggerated emphasis, declamation and gesture are quite unnecessary; the pieces chosen are to be read with feeling and intelligence, but they are not to be acted' (p. 36).

As more Handbooks were published each decade and more government sponsored reports such as Hadow (1926–31) and Primary School (1931) emerged, official support for Drama in schools, both formal and informal, grew. What they all have in common, however, is an inclination to see improvement in speech as one of the chief educational reasons for giving children a diet of drama. Perhaps this represented an effort on their part not to take sides between formal and informal drama, practice in speech being seen as common to both. This emphasis which the committees themselves may not have been conscious of creating, was of enormous significance. It willy-nilly introduced a new concept – that of *training* in a specific skill. Even though speech practitioners persisted in seeing their work as child-centred and concerned with personal development, their focus on training could not be denied. Ken Robinson (1981) quotes from one teacher who is concerned with:

> ... giving children a rudimentary dramatic training in speech and movement in the belief that the exercise of such a training has a benefit of its own (p. 51).

Now the official reports in some ways were doing no more than reflecting a new movement that was going on outside the normal education system. Battalions (well, perhaps not the right word!) of elocution teachers were infiltrating our towns and cities and private lessons in speech-training was becoming a big industry – which supplies us with a name to attach to this movement – that of Elsie Fogerty (1920). Tim Cox (1970) writes of Miss Fogerty in the following terms:

> Miss Fogerty was concerned throughout her life with the improvement of speech and as a pioneer in speech therapy she opened her first clinic in St. Thomas's Hospital in 1912. In 1889, at the age of twenty-four, she was appointed lecturer in English and Speech at the Crystal Palace School of Art and Literature and later she taught in south-eastern schools. She founded the Central School of Speech Training and Dramatic Art in 1906. For a long time she tried to obtain university recognition for her Speech Therapy School and succeeded in 1923 when it was approved as a training place for the newly-instituted London University Diploma in Dramatic Art (p. 53).

This dynamic lady brought respectability to a new

profession of speech-trainers. She and her close supporters, Sir Henry Newbolt, Sir Ben Greet, Sir Sidney Lee (what a prestigious, titled bunch!) influenced the opening of specialist colleges. One of the functions of such colleges as Trinity, Royal Academy of Music and Drama and Guildhall became that of examining board to the private speech teaching that proliferated (and is still going strong today) throughout the country – and the empire! Many such teachers emigrated to Australia and South Africa in particular where they held, for example, prestigious posts in teacher-training institutions. The British Drama League was formed in the early 1920s to be followed by the Association of Teachers of Speech and Drama in the 1930s.

Alongside this growth in speech work was the huge amateur theatre movement with its emphasis on bigger and better productions and through the British Drama League, competitive Play Festivals, Poetry and Choral Speech Festivals were popularised. Many of the personnel connected with this amateur movement were themselves teachers in our schools, so that the idea of raising standards of performance by training in speech and, logically enough, *acting* seemed a natural extension to classroom drama. Training in speech, acting and mime became a not uncommon feature of drama even with our youngest children, so that many teachers who had hitherto been happily trying out the dramatic method of teaching in our elementary schools handed over to the 'expert', for drama was now becoming something they thought they were not capable of teaching. Indeed, it is significant that those teachers in the profession who wanted to be recognised as experts could only show a qualification in their subject by taking the various licentiate examinations referred to above. This was true right up until the 1950s when the Drama Board added its own qualification, but even after that date the prestige attached to Licentiates of the Royal Academy or of Guildhall has persisted, so that for instance when I was appointed as drama adviser to a local authority as late as 1962, I was told that my appointment was on the strength of my having an L.R.A.M., a qualification which by that date had little to do with the work I was appointed to advise on!

Perhaps the tone set by the new movement for expertise in speech and drama is best captured by the Association of Teachers of Speech and Drama's declared objects as stated in 1952. I am grateful to Ken Robinson (1981) for the following quotation from the Association's constitution:

... To protect the professional interests of members and to promote the advancement of knowledge, study and practice of speech and dramatic art in every form.

To secure the proper educational status of Spoken English in schools, colleges and teachers' training establishments, to ensure that those teaching speech training are properly qualified and to encourage artistic use and appreciation of good speech (p. 53).

Summary

I have suggested that drama, like other subjects qualifying for a place in the school curriculum, has been part of a continual polarisation between two distinct views of education: knowledge-centred and child-centred. It is unlikely that either of these could exist in a pure form. Nevertheless because drama is by definition action based, it represented for some educators associated with the so-called New Education movement part of their vision of what progressive education could look like. I offered this as a reason why teachers using drama have persisted in identifying themselves as advocates of child-centredness and self-expression when in practice the energising centre of their work has been in another direction. In the case of Harriet Finlay-Johnson it was towards the objective world of facts. In Caldwell Cook's work it was towards the craft of the artist. The orientation of the speech experts was towards training in a specific skill. An underlying assumption perhaps all the early pioneers shared which place them firmly within the Romantic movement of Education was that drama somehow put children in touch with the spiritual side of themselves. This view of dramatic activity as a natural force for good we shall meet in the next chapter when we look at the work of Peter Slade.

2 The middle of the twentieth century

Peter Slade and the Speech and Drama experts

This educational giant, Peter Slade, began his career in the theatre and the irony of fate is such that he started a powerful anti-theatre movement among his followers without having had the slightest intention of doing so. In his major publication, *Child Drama* (1954), Peter Slade makes it very clear that he sees formal theatre as a final stage in a child's development. Because he is aware of possible dangers in that stage of development being imposed too soon and because he gives most of his attention in the book to helping teachers find an alternative approach for young children, people have erroneously assumed that he is against theatre.

It is not surprising that this happened, for in the 1940s and 1950s dichotomisation was in the air. Harriet Finlay-Johnson and Caldwell Cook had found it easy to embrace both improvised and scripted drama into their work without apparently realising there was an issue to be faced, although they both eschewed 'artificial' acting. Harriet Finlay-Johnson recalls, 'One remembers the "actions" taught in lessons set apart for "recitation" and "action" songs. How little they expressed what the child itself felt' (pp. 54–55). But the speech and acting training movement had, in the thirty or so intervening years since Miss Johnson wrote these words, given respectability to taught actions, gestures and spoken expression. Teachers found they were under pressure to take sides. Either one was for the refined expression of the stage or, as it seemed to the 'experts', one was for the free expression of children's own colloquial banalities.

Peter Slade had his first teaching experience, according

to a letter written to Tim Cox (1970), with 'backward children in Worcestershire' (p. 253) in the late 1930s. By the time he was ready to give public voice to his theories of Child Drama, growing hostility to anything that smacked of free expression provided a less than receptive climate for his ideas. One of the major problems was that the Speech and Drama experts were offering their particular brand of training in the name of child-centred and experiential education. 'For clearly,' they could argue, 'drama is *doing*; it is demonstrably active education in keeping with the Hadow (1931) recommendation that education was about "activity and experience rather than knowledge to be acquired and facts to be stored".'

Thus Peter Slade was faced with the bizarre task of attempting to sell progressive education to people who thought they were the ones who were already pioneering it. No wonder they thought he was a crank! Two factors led them to believe they were progressive. One was the continual battle they were waging to break the suspicion of traditional teachers who saw drama as interfering with the proper work of imparting facts. (The empty pitcher model of education dies hard and, of course, has come strongly into favour again today with our current bias towards public examinations.) The other factor was that they saw themselves as missionaries bringing the arts and our cultural heritage to children whose lives were barren of these civilising things. And indeed they had a right to see themselves in this light. Some outstanding school play productions are evidence of the worthiness of their aims. It is to be regretted that this form of school celebration has suffered as a result of alternative philosophies of drama in education.

Thus these liberators of the school curriculum, speaking the language of child-centredness, of activity, of personal growth, of spiritual uplift, of feelings, of learning by doing and of group co-operation, in facing squarely the traditionalists in our classrooms opposed to drama as an unnecessary pastime, found themselves attacked from behind, as it were, by this City of Birmingham local education authority adviser (as Peter Slade became in 1947) who talked his own peculiar language but seemingly with the same intention of promoting dramatic activity in the classroom. To them one of his more unpalatable 'deviations' was his insistence that the activity was not for showing. This could only be seen as illogical, for drama more than any other art form was about communication and indeed the very substance of drama teaching was training in communication skills.

Thus we have in a nutshell why within our educational system in the 1940s, 1950s and 1960s two sets of teachers, both groups allied to progressiveness in education through drama, could find no basis for speaking to each other. I say 'groups' for Peter Slade soon gathered devotees around him, although his career has been punctuated by a series of historical occasions (the Bonnington Hotel Conference in 1948 perhaps marked the watershed of the dichotomisation of drama in education) when he has stood alone against a line-up of his fellow advisers whose vested interest was in training children to perform. We shall be returning to this important turning-point in drama in education's history in Chapter Four.

To understand what Peter Slade was alarmed about when he observed the work of Speech and Drama teachers (a label which I shall continue to give them for convenience, although it may not always be accurate as, for instance, some teachers taught speech or mime only, and, of course, I am using the term to apply not just to drama specialists but to all teachers of all ages who include this more formal training in drama within their curriculum), we have to look closely at what was understood by dramatic action or acting behaviour, not at this stage with a view to definition but to identify some of its characteristics. Peter Slade's theories are based on a particular kind of acting behaviour which differed markedly from that approved by Speech and Drama teachers. It is central to this brief historical survey and to the whole thesis of this book that we attempt to distinguish such modes of behaviour.

24

The performing mode

Speech and Drama teachers were not inventing a cause, they were responding to a real need on two fronts – the cultural impoverishment of many of our children and a marked lack of ability to communicate outside their own immediate circle. Speech-training seemed the obvious way of helping the latter. Unfortunately experts of the time could not have access to the developed understanding of 'language in context' that we have today, so that much effort was spent on imposing a speech style (often 'received', 'standard' or 'B.B.C.' speech) on children, a kind of external grafting that had little to do with the pupils' own expressiveness, but nevertheless created a convention of speaking (and moving) that, although artificial, in the very process of being conventionalised became the norm – affectation was accepted and expected. And motivated pupils, forever good mimics, adopted what was required and enjoyed the subsequent adult approval.

Ability to communicate is a very personal thing and with the proliferation of private Speech and Drama teaching, giving children such individual attention, the practice of publicly reciting a poem or, more significantly, of reciting dialogue from a play with no other players around created not only a new convention, but totally revolutionised the conception of a play's performance which from Caldwell Cook's example had been to do with a group of pupils communicating to an audience the events of a play. Now the stress was to be on an individual actor's ability to communicate a character's dialogue to an audience. In other words there was a subtle switch from 'drama is about a play' to 'drama is about *me* in a play' – and much showing-off we got as a result.

A further distortion can be detected. Speech and Drama teachers were properly conscious of standards and naturally enough people in the business of training children to perform used the professional theatre as its yardstick. Unfortunately, the theatre of the 1930s, 1940s and

1950s did not always offer the best examples of theatre. The West End was often flooded with 'french-window' plays published in French's acting editions. Just as in the U.S.A. the popularity of musicals in American theatre is reflected by a similar choice in their schools, so our schools were inundated with sets of plays written especially for children and filled with inconsequential escapist drama. The *content* of plays or speech exercises was of little importance – it was *doing* them that mattered.

But there was a more subtle influence from the professional theatre itself than its escapism and that was its *naturalism*. The art of acting as it was understood in this period was to make the performance seem as externally real as possible – 'real' french windows had to be matched by 'real' butlers with trays answering 'real' telephones. This is not to be confused, however, with the extreme interpretations of the so-called 'Method' acting of the 1960s where the actors tried on stage *not* to act (a contradiction of terms if ever there was one!) so that the audience was, as it were, incidentally present at what was going on. Naturalism was the reverse of this. It was a sophisticated convention for projecting (to the back of the gallery) a resemblance of the detail of everyday actions. Just as students across the Atlantic might well be applauded for clever foot-work in dancing the Charleston ready for *The Boyfriend*, so our pupils were applauded for the clarity with which they artificially conveyed naturalistic behaviour. We have suffered from generations of teachers and pupils who have thought that learning to act was to do with acquiring the clichés of naturalism. Only in recent years in this country have more healthy approaches to performance modes been tried out. I am thinking of the work of Albert Hunt (1976) as a good example of what I mean.

What Peter Slade was requiring of children in schools was that they changed their preconceptions of acting behaviour, that they found again the acting mode that was natural to them. If it was difficult for teachers to conceive of an alternative mode, it was bewildering to children to find that their acquired conventional styles were no longer approved of. It is noticeable that children trained over a period of time in conventionalised acting find it very difficult to be natural and spontaneous even when there is no-one else watching, and many of our children still resort to performance clichés when they go into small groups to improvise. (It was disappointing that the Schools Council (1977) observers did not comment on this particular 'hybrid' convention.) Likewise teachers who of course have accepted it over a number of years no longer 'see' it.

But this emphasis on the importance of the resemblance of things is more insidious than an artificial acting style. It undermines the very essence of the art form of theatre. Theatre is nothing if it does not deal in powerful symbols. That it is both concrete *and* symbolic is what distinguishes it from the other arts. If the symbolic element is taken away, as naturalistic theatre tends to do, theatre's life-blood has been removed. Our children and teachers have inherited an anaemic conception of dramatic art as imitation of concrete actions. Responding to and creating symbols, the very basis of all work in art, has been neglected. This perhaps above all else is the most serious indictment of the Speech and Drama approach. The great leaders in this field are not to be blamed for this neglect, but in the process of proliferation of individualised training understanding the very nature of the art form became eroded.

The dramatic playing mode

If the tone of approval applied by some educators to child-centred education was thought to be overly romantic, then the way some benign writers on child play approached their subject could only be described as rhapsodical. Drama exponents interested in the value of dramatic play

27

have tended to echo the euphoric idealistic views expressed by Froebel (1912) who saw play as 'the highest expression of human development in childhood, for it alone is the free expression of what is in the child's soul' (pp. 50–51). As Tim Cox has pointed out, one of the first writers to take particular interest in make-believe play as opposed to play in general was James Sully who in 1896 wrote:

> We talk ... glibly about their play, their make-believe, their illusions; but how much do we really know of their state of mind when they act out a little scene of domestic life or of the battle-field? (p. 322)

Sully further anticipated Slade by drawing parallels between the development of the child in make-believe and the development of primitive art. He boldly distinguishes dramatic play from performance:

> The scenes he acts out ... are not produced as having objective value, but rather as providing himself with a new environment ... The idea of a child playing as an actor is said to 'play' in order to delight others is a contradiction in terms ... the pleasure of a child in what we call 'dramatic' make-believe is wholly independent of any appreciating eye (p. 326).

Writing nearly twenty years later, Joseph Lee (1915) tentatively identifies the developmental stages in play, a perspective which Peter Slade was later to expand and refine. Lee also anticipated Slade in attempting to isolate the very elements of play – its basic rhythms, its sense of space, and, above all, the power of symbolic shapes such as the ring. It is a curious turn of events that by the mid-century when Speech and Drama exponents were inadvertently eroding a consciousness in children of symbolism in theatre, Peter Slade was helping teachers to re-find a universal symbolism in a child's exploratory play. He writes:

> The constant repetitions and use of symbols in the

realm of child behaviour, also the acting out of situations sometimes before they can have been experienced, is entirely in line with the Jungian conception of the collective unconscious. We find story themes concerned with birth, marriage, parenthood, death and resurrection. All dolls and treasures are, in a manner, babies; weddings always come into dramatic play, as do mothers and fathers, and people who are killed but often get up again (resurrection). We also hear references to the hereafter and to eternity, and at five years there is already apparent a certain recognition of good and evil, or at least of opposing forces (p. 48).

Both Lee and Slade emphasise the symbolic importance of the circle or ring. Those of us who are practitioners in drama can sense in our bones just how right they are to stress this. (One only has to observe the tension felt by children who are left on the outside of a ring compared with those who are protected from within it. For young children or immature adults reaching the 'safety' of the circle may be a strong motivating factor that the most egocentric individuals find they can share). Joseph Lee expresses it eloquently:

> There is in the ring game the sense of belonging to a social whole . . . We feel and care about the ring itself. There is a sense of personal loss if it gets broken – to have it squashed in on one side gives a sense of impaired personality . . . and we hasten in such case with much squealing, to mend or round it out again. The ring is now a part of us, as we of it . . . It is an extension of ourselves, a new personality; we act now not as individuals, but as the ring; its success is our success and what hits it hits us. The ring, like the family, is a social whole. (p. 139)

For me the above passage by Joseph Lee not only epitomises the power of the art form in drama but also identifies those characteristics which distinguish the collective arts such as drama and dance from the individual arts such as painting and poetry. (It is significant, too, as we shall be discussing later, that Lee is describing not drama itself but a *game*).

But there is, however, a symbolic way of looking at a circle that is *not* collective. Peter Slade was very much influenced by contemporary interest in child-centred art education and acknowledges the work of Professor Cizek and his English interpreter W. Viola (1942) who attaches importance to a remark made about the meaning of a circle by William Stern in 1908:

> Every man experiences himself as the centre of the space surrounding himself, but this space is only conquered by steps.

This conception of a child at the centre of his own circle struggling to master it lacks the social connotations of Lee's interpretation. Slade is intrigued by evidence of this 'private circle' – he draws our attention to the individual's attempt to draw his own personal circle through dipping his finger in spittle or paint, through crawling in circles, through gesture and dancing (p. 25), although he does go on to acknowledge the importance of the group circle. Nevertheless I sense an ambivalence here that has raised a fundamental issue for drama teaching. Whatever Peter Slade's intentions have been, I would suggest that in the main what people have taken from him is his concern with the child's 'personal circle', that Child Drama is their supreme example of child-centred activity. It could well be the case that in the two interpretations of the circle we have here (and, may I say, I am most grateful to Tim Cox for his discernment in making this point in his thesis), we have revealed a critical juncture in the history of drama in education. Lee's interpretation could have led to a theoretical elaboration which emphasised the collective 'game' of drama. The interpretation adopted by Slade and his followers (particularly Brian Way) has taken Child Drama along the path of individualisation which, as we have seen, for very different reasons, Speech and Drama exponents also followed. It was Dorothy Heathcote who

30

some forty years after Lee's publication attempted (although it was a long time before she was listened to) to restate the importance of the collective experience and in doing so brought again to the fore the possibility of group members becoming united in their shared response to dramatic symbols – but more of this later. Although Peter Slade espoused the symbolism of Jung, his emphasis on the importance of the individual led teachers, if they were conscious of symbols at all, to focus on the symbolism of the clinic rather than of the theatre. Thus begins the trend still with us today (see, for instance, two huge volumes published in 1981 by Gertrud Schattner and Richard Courtney) of drama teachers seeing at least part of their function as that of therapist – which gives another ironic twist to this history, for Peter Slade was at pains to make a clear distinction between the two. He writes:

> . . . and I would go so far as to say that one of the most important reasons for developing Child Drama in schools generally is not actually a therapeutic one, *but the even more constructive one of prevention* (p. 119).

In practice most of Peter Slade's followers were not ready to grasp the symbolic content of Child Drama. 'Drama is doing' became their catch-phrase (as it was the Speech and Drama teachers') and creating the opportunity for 'spontaneous doing' was what a teacher concerned himself with.

I have called this form of activity 'dramatic playing'. The term 'make-believe' play would have done just as well. However I intend to use 'dramatic playing' in a particular way which needs an explanation here. Most writers on drama in education, including Peter Slade and Brian Way, have found a terminology to describe the *activity* itself. They both refer to performance as an identifiable kind of event or relationship with an audience. For Peter Slade, 'play' means spontaneous action and, as we shall see, Brian Way uses the term 'exercise' for a variety of structured activities. I have chosen to highlight, as I did in my previous publication (1979), not the activity itself but the *disposition* or *mental set* appropriate to the activity, for I believe this to be the key to understanding the underlying experience. The criterion I have used for classifying these dispositional modes is that of *intention*. 'Dramatic playing' is an *intention to be*, to be in a different environment or context from the one actually present. 'Performance mode' refers to the *intention to communicate* to an audience, that is, to describe to someone outside the make-believe. Whereas 'dramatic playing' is an intention to be in an imaginary event, 'performance mode' is the intention to describe an imaginary event.

Peter Slade believes the two essential qualities of the 'dramatic playing' disposition are absorption and sincerity. He defines them as follows:

> Absorption – being completely wrapped up in what is being done or what one is doing, to the exclusion of all thoughts, including the awareness of or desire for an audience (p. 12).

> Sincerity – a complete form of honesty in portraying a part, bringing with it an intense feeling of reality and experience ... and only fully achieved in the process of acting with absorption (p. 14).

I shall later in the book wish to add to these features and perhaps qualify them, but for the present let them stand as the guidelines they were to young teachers like me who tried to work towards these qualities in the drama lesson. We measured our success by the degrees of absorption and sincerity we could observe. Slade gives an example of what he means by Child Drama. For him the following extract epitomises high-quality work:

> The teacher has in the earlier part of this lesson with 5–6 year-olds given the children some movement experiences to piano accompaniment. She then suggests 'Parties' to them. Peter Slade continues his description: 'Circles of three or four children formed all over the

room (no music). They were left entirely alone and began to eat or pour out tea. Some unwrapped parcels. One little girl tidied her friend's hair, another smoothed her frock and danced to the others in her little group.

TEACHER (*timing it carefully*) 'A postman brings toys. Would that be nice?'
ALL THE CHILDREN 'Yes.'

Two or three boys became postmen. The teacher saw that she had created the right atmosphere for Child Drama, and ceased to guide the class. She backed quietly into a corner. The boys moved to one side of the room and suddenly turned themselves into lorries. (Taking letters? Probably. They may have been post vans by mental association, but their noise was that of a heavy lorry. Note the Child experience not fully developed, perhaps. Something to watch. When will they give us post vans that sound like vans? Or do letters go by lorry in their 'land'? The teacher might suggest 'vans' in the weeks ahead, without any suggestion that lorries are wrong, and see whether the noise changes.) Some of the lorries (and/or vans) changed into trains and then *a* train. Others became aeroplanes.

This was the moment of real Child Theatre. Five excellently placed rings of little girls remained absorbedly eating and pouring out tea. The four postmen were in one corner, on an imaginary platform. The train had formed on the other side of the room, preparatory to running round the whole playing space in one large circle.

Lorries were driving towards the train between the tea-parties and behind the postmen; inter-crossing waves of six and six aeroplanes were weaving a snake-wise dance in the space left, their arms outstretched and banking as they ran. (Excellent example of 'running play').

I longed for a gallery to see from. This is what we should realise. The Child creates theatre in its own way, own form, own kind. It is original art of high creative quality. Most adults are stubbornly blind to the loveliness they will not see (p. 183).

I have quoted the above at length for it tells the reader not only about Slade's conception of Child Drama, but about the man himself. In this extract we can feel the excitement and joy of this man who looks at children in this loving way and who wants us to see what he sees – and many of us tried. We soon discovered that children will only play in this free way when there is trust – of each other and of the teacher. And it need not be confined to young children. Adolescents, given the right conditions, will eagerly play. I can recall a group of fourteen-year-olds, given a whole afternoon of drama, set up their 'Japanese war' environment and 'played' continuously without any teacher interruption for one and a half hours. And indeed adults sometimes enjoy such playing. I remember on one occasion in the late 1960s, daring to interrupt a group of teachers who were trying to absorb themselves in the life of a primitive tribe, only to be firmly told by them that I was 'ruining their creativity'. For continuously sustained dramatic playing became for some followers of Peter Slade the hall-mark of good drama.

The teacher is not to be seen as a teacher, but rather as a 'loving ally' assisting in the natural expression of his pupils. This is a very difficult thing to be, for one of the principal differences between a professional teacher and an amateur such as a classroom helper or a baby-minder is that a teacher has some notion of direction. But Slade has removed from the professional such common supports as immediate goals and objectives (Harriet Finlay-Johnson always had a set of facts to be learned and the Speech and Drama experts had their set of skills to be taught). The Sladian teacher can only reach towards vague long-term aspirations. Faced with a class of nine-year-olds, he may not derive much comfort from Slade's claim that 'cleanliness, tidiness, gracefulness, politeness, cheerfulness, confidence, ability to mix, thoughtfulness for others, discrimination, moral discernment, honesty and loyalty, ability to lead companions, reliability, and a readiness to remain steadfast under difficulties, appear to be the result of correct and prolonged Drama training' (p. 125).

The activity of Child Drama appeared to be without content and without form and the drama lesson without structure apart from a loose sequence of relaxing and releasing activity followed by unfettered dramatic playing. Surely this is Romantic child-centredness at its purest. Peter Slade's books (1954, 1958) are indeed probably the nearest any individual has reached in giving a practical form to the Rousseauesque conception of education – which may cause the reader to wonder why I insisted in the first chapter that drama in education has never really embraced the philosophy of pure self-expression.

Peter Slade gave young teachers like myself a loophole, a way out of feeling redundant. He invented what he called 'The Ideas Game', which he intended should be used sparingly as but one of many ways of getting things going. 'It should be understood,' he warned, 'that this game ... is only useful in that form for *beginning* things.' But because it let the teachers off the hook of working in apparent formlessness, it became popularised as *the* Sladian method. I again propose to quote at length for in my view it represents a distortion of the educational drama process which has continued to block our understanding ever since.

The Ideas Game

... 'It is one that I have made up and have used with all ages from infants to adults. Ask one or two people (or Children) to give you an idea in one or a few words – 'What's in your mind?' – sometimes you can't think of anything – 'Well, did you come here on a 'bus – did you notice anything, anyone *on* the 'bus?'

CHILD   Blue hat.

SELF   All right, thank you – blue hat. Now someone else – you?

CHILD Please sir, food.

ANOTHER CHILD Umbrella.

SELF Yes. All right, thank you. Now we have three ideas; blue hat, food, umbrella. Will you help me to remember them? (Child-teacher relationship). Once upon a time there was a funny old man and he lived in a funny old house, over there *in that corner*, and there were two things which he wanted very much in the shops – *over there* (in another corner), but he was very poor and he couldn't afford them. But they were: (1) food; (2) a blue hat. And he didn't know which to get. But he shuffled out of his little house, down the winding road (all over in the middle of the space, *there* you see), and by the road were *trees*, which bent towards him as he passed, saying, each in turn, 'Good morning, old man, good morning'. But when he got to the shops it began to rain, and he *did* want a blue hat and he *did* want some food, but suddenly he saw – what?

EVERYONE An umbrella.

SELF Yes, he saw a wonderful umbrella, and he went in and bought it with his last penny. But he didn't know it was a magic one, and he *couldn't* help wishing he had his blue hat too, and he was very hungry. But what do you think happened when he got home (the house can be made of twenty or thirty human bricks if necessary) – he found that by wishing with the umbrella in his hands his friends the trees had found him two presents. What were they?

ALL Food – blue hat.

SELF Yes, and he put the hat straight on although he was in the house; not very polite, but the trees said he might just for once. And they all leaned over him, and filled him and filled him with so much food that he slowly went – to – sleep and all the trees passed quietly out of the house and rustled back to their places. There you are, you made it all up didn't you – just from three ideas? (They didn't of course – you did. But they helped, and the ideas stimulate one's imagination.) Now

36

let's act it, and you shall add some more ideas. (Improvisation starts, mimed or with their words.) (p. 145)

That the above story is the teacher's does not worry me, as Peter Slade only saw it as a temporary measure towards children making up the story themselves. There are, however, two features about which we need to show some concern. (There may be others about which to express concern or delight, but my purpose is not to give a detailed analysis of Slade's philosophy and practice – only to draw attention to selected features.) One is to do with the mental disposition that this particular form of acting behaviour requires; the second is to do with the implicit assumption about what drama is.

Let us remind ourselves of the disposition of 'dramatic playing' as described above: it is essentially *being* or *existential*. There is a critical sense of 'it is happening now' and 'I do not know this present moment's future'. I can *guess* what might happen as I do in moment-to-moment living, but I cannot *know* it. Now if a teacher uses the above sequence of building up a story followed by enactment (Peter Slade recommended the teacher should narrate during the enactment, leading the children through the complexities of the story), the experience is *not* 'dramatic playing'. The existential experience of the lesson has in fact already occurred as the pupils heard the story evolve. When they get on their feet to act, the quality of being becomes modified by the intention to describe in action the story they have just heard – it is now a 're-collection' requiring representation as if it is a product, and secondly, by a subtle shift of perspective on time, 'what is happening now' becomes overshadowed by 'what we know will happen next'. The child does not engage with the present moment, but rather with moving to the next moment. 'What happens next' becomes the controlling mental set.

Thus what appears to be self-expression through dramatic playing is critically re-orientated towards a

37

disposition to describe and to foreshadow. Here once again we have an example of a hybrid form of acting behaviour which although empirically observable (one of its characteristics in practice is the highly condensed form the action takes – just the opposite from dramatic playing which tends to become more and more protracted) has not been acknowledged. Let me make it clear that I am not condemning it because it is hybrid – indeed later in the book we shall be looking at certain hybrid forms that have distinct educational advantages – but because it is a particularly limited mode of expression which a lack of sophistication on the part of teachers has led erroneously to its being given the Child Drama accolade. Peter Slade, of course, recognised its limitations and encouraged children to improvise within it – but this is extremely difficult to do because it requires the children to 'change gear', or to be using both gears at the same time. Where of course it can happen is when only the first half of the story is built up beforehand (Peter Slade also recommended this method), in which case the sequence becomes (1) hearing the story, (2) a hybrid mode of representation and (3) dramatic playing.

Please do not assume that because for the moment I seem to have slipped into discussing a particular method of teaching that I am particularly supportive of the enactment of stories. I am using this example of methodology merely to once more make the point that what may look like self-expression is far from being so. There has indeed been a danger which I want to discuss now of teachers seeing Peter Slade's 'Ideas Game' as giving a stamp of approval to the popular representation of stories, a view which Slade does nothing to discourage. Shakespeare understood that plots are not in themselves what drama is about: they are merely the retrospective link between situations. It is *in retrospect* that a play tells a story. As it unfolds, the audience is identifying with the occurring situation. Likewise, in make-believe play, a child can play at, say, Cowboys and Indians, and it is *afterward* that he could reformulate the action of his playing into a story form.

A large number of teachers seem to have misunderstood both theatre and play: they have appreciated that drama by its very nature is action bound, but have assumed that has meant the sequential actions of plot rather than the inner dynamic of a situation. Thus teachers' observations of their own class's drama has often been tied to the 'what-happens-next' perspective. In placing the emphasis on getting the plot right, they have entirely overlooked the fundamental nature of the art. And in so doing they have, of course, to go back to our original metaphor, firmly taken the centre of gravity away from the child to the plot.

There is not space here to give Peter Slade's theories the full attention which they deserve. I am obliged to confine myself to selecting those aspects which seem in my view to have most affected the educational assumptions behind teachers' practice. There is, however, another important aspect of his theory to which I shall be referring in Chapter Six. This is his classification of play into 'personal' and 'projected' play. It has taken me many years to appreciate the fundamental significance of this particular form of classification. Easier to grasp are those kind of categories used by play theorists – for instance Piaget's (1926) division into practice play, symbolic play, and games with rules. The relevance for the teacher of Slade's classification is not so apparent. Without going into details now, I would like to make the point that the recognition of these two distinct behaviours which form the very basis of his theories provides us with a rationale for drama education which has hitherto not been understood.

This chapter began with a discussion of why supporters of Peter Slade could find little in common with the Speech and Drama exponents. A body which did not belong or wish to belong to either camp was, of course, the Ministry of Education. Let me finish this chapter with two quotations I have picked up from Ken Robinson (1981) who has had access to an unpublished yet nevertheless very important document written by a working party on drama in schools in 1949. Ken Robinson quotes that there is no place in schools,

> ... for the ruthless producer whose artistic egoism leads him to regard children as so many puppets, to be moved about according to some design of his own (p. 46).

Neither is there a place,

> ... for the sentimentalist who has unproved theories on pure 'self-expression' (p. 4).

Thus we have an official attempt to put a brake on dichotomisation!

Summary

In this chapter we have dipped into the philosophy and practice of Peter Slade. His valiant attempts to create a genuine Child Drama have to be seen against the background of a Speech and Drama movement that was pulling in the opposite direction, although both parties saw themselves as pioneers in progressive education.

While acknowledging what the latter group of experts have done for the school play, and expressing my considerable respect for Slade's vision, I have teased out those aspects of both approaches which have in my view led in practice to some kind of distortion of what the pioneers originally intended.

I have suggested that both sides have given undue emphasis to individualisation; the Speech and Drama people because of the necessity of training, the Sladian followers because of the importance attached to personal expression. I have suggested that both have distorted the nature of the dramatic medium, the former by emphasising naturalism, the latter by stressing that aspect of drama to do with story-line.

I have discussed performance and dramatic playing as dispositions rather than as activities, and have suggested that when children enact a known story-line this only *appears* to harness the dramatic playing disposition, that in fact it focuses away from the very kind of expressive behaviour teachers purport to be encouraging.

3   The 1960s and 1970s

Brian Way and Dorothy Heathcote

Since a whole book could be written about the professional work of each of these innovators, there is a danger that in the process of selection I shall distort or over-simplify. Indeed, I have blundered straight away by placing them in a context of the 1960s and 1970s, as though in 1970 they stopped! I have not seen Brian Way for a few years now, since he went to work in America, but if he is continually developing his philosophy and practice at the rate Dorothy Heathcote is refining hers, then there is the added danger that anything written about them is out of date as it leaves the press.

Give or take a few years they are contemporaries, and yet historically people place Brian Way very much earlier. This is partly because he became known much sooner. When colleges of education in the 1960s were clamouring to employ Brian Way as their external examiner and his children's theatre companies were a household name throughout the country's education authorities, Dorothy Heathcote was relatively unknown in spite of having held her university post since the early 1950s. I first met Brian in 1958 and Dorothy just three years later. Both have had an enormous impact on me as a teacher. One of the things they taught me was to be independent of doctrine, for their separate advice to me was contradictory.

It is the fascination of these contrasted views of drama in education that I would like to share with the reader as the basis for this chapter. What these two exponents have in common is their deep concern for the education of children and their considerable reservations about what goes on in the name of education in our present institutions. And both of them use drama as a process for children's enrichment – but here the similarity ceases. Indeed, if you were to ask each what he or she infers from the term enrichment in this context, the divergence of their thinking may become apparent straight away. Whereas Brian Way's answer might be that drama helps with 'the release of the real me' (1981), Dorothy Heathcote's might place 'stumbling on authenticity' (1980) high on her list of enrichments.

Brian Way

A close associate of Peter Slade in their early pioneering days, Brian Way developed the philosophy and methodology of Child Drama along a broader front. His work embraced children's theatre, classroom drama and the integrated arts. It may well be that it is the first of these, his work in children's theatre, for which he will be most remembered, for he revolutionised the whole conception of what forms theatre for children might take. Just as Peter Slade had to stand up against a tradition of formalised children's drama, so Brian Way had to educate teachers into understanding that children deserved something better than light entertainment. The history of children's theatre and Theatre in Education (as it is now called), with its own nice mixture of educational thinkers as its leaders – Bertha Waddell, Caryl Jenner, Gerald Tyler, Gordon Vallins, Stuart Bennett, Roger Chapman, Cora Williams, John O'Toole (1976), David Pammeter, Pam Schweitzer, Geoff Gillham and Tony Jackson (1980), to select a few – to a considerable extent reflects the changing conception of drama in the classroom during these two decades. If anything, Theatre in Education tends to be ahead of drama in education. There is unfortunately not the space here to include such a history, but merely to reiterate that what Brian Way was offering schools in the 1950s and 1960s was far ahead of his contemporaries in the field. Perhaps his best known innovation, audience participation, is now well documented in his most recent publication (1981) – that we now take audience participation for granted is almost entirely due to the pioneering work of this very able teacher and director.

But we have to examine his other main passion: creative drama, as it came to be called round about this time. He had a big advantage over Peter Slade in that by the time his seminal publication, *Development through Drama*, emerged in 1967, the profession, particularly teachers in the Primary schools, was more eager to seize upon his message. As John Deverall (1979) points out, in that same year our Plowden Committee published its stamp of approval on progressive education. Child-centred education, at least in the Primary schools, was now seen to be respectable. Teacher-training institutions were expanding and many of Brian Way's devotees were appointed to lead new drama courses. (It might be useful to remind the reader at this point that the Speech and Drama movement, although fading at the school level, had become firmly entrenched in teacher colleges where many well qualified Speech and Drama people had gained appointments, colleges such as Trent Park and Goldsmiths', where teacher-training in the arts was not unlike theatre-training.) Through Brian Way's influence a new kind of college course was emerging that saw drama as the basis for the students' own personal development. Perhaps the most impressive of these was Loughborough College where that fine, sensitive associate of Peter Slade and Brian Way, Stan Evernden, was the first lecturer to evolve a student-centred drama course for potential teachers. Indeed the first handbook of drama based on Peter Slade's philosophy emerged from this college where Pemberton-Billing (1965), a tutor there, joined forces with David Clegg, a student.

The training of teachers in how to teach drama requires

some kind of formula. *Development through Drama* seemed to provide just this and became a set text worldwide, but as with most formulae, the recommended practice often does not quite match the philosophy. Curious contradictions can creep in. When one watches Brian Way teach a class of children, as I have had the privilege to do, one has a strong sense of coherence in theory and practice, but what people take from a theoretical book can often be a distortion of what was actually intended by the author. I do not suppose, for instance, that Brian Way imagined that teachers would adopt a 'shopping-list' method of conducting lessons based on a few arbitrarily chosen activities strung together for children to respond to in rapid succession. (Just as, in the case of my own work, I did not anticipate that some teachers would begin every lesson with 'What do you want to do a play about?'. These misinterpretations can become embedded in practice and, once there, are difficult to eradicate.)

Let us look at some of the assumptions implicit in 'creative drama'. There are four in particular that have significant educational implications: (1) the emphasis on individualisation, (2) the encouragement of the 'exercise' disposition or mode of behaviour, (3) the widening of activities to be embraced by drama, and (4) the importance of intuition, which I shall discuss under the section heading 'Dorothy Heathcote'.

1 Individualisation
In carrying the banner for the 'uniqueness of the individual', Brian Way has been seen as an articulate and effective militant against the authoritarian stance of traditional education. Although his writings may not have had the breadth of impact of his 'human growth' contemporaries across the Atlantic, such as Carl Rogers (1961) and Abraham Maslow (1954), it is possible that because he offered an unpretentious dramatic model, teachers found his approach more immediately accessible than Rogers' ideology. It may be, too, that Way's essential

practicality helped to deflect some of the more sensational encounter-group and psychodrama-type experiments from the British drama scene.

But the obvious drawback to emphasising the importance of the individual is that it can lead to unhealthy egocentrism. If the pupil in the drama lesson is conscious of using drama to help 'the real me to get out' then this could be as limiting as the most inflexible authoritarian teaching. John Deverall (1979), in a fascinating but as yet unpublished dissertation on the 'Public Medium/Private Process' dichotomy, draws our attention to authors such as Richard Sennett (1974) and Iris Murdoch (1970), the former deploring the cult of the individual in modern society and the latter arguing fiercely for the arts as 'unselfing'. And recently, in education, we have David Hargreaves (1982) pointing out the harm done in schools when the balance of attention is given to the individuals rather than to the group – and this from a non-authoritarian, liberal educationalist. Such a view begins to turn on its head the old assumption that individualism is the *sine qua non* of progressive education.

And I wish to argue further that in using drama to promote the individual's growth we have inadvertently distorted drama itself on two counts. The first is that drama is never about oneself; it is always concerned with something outside oneself. And secondly, drama is a social event not a solitary experience. It is one thing to claim that by sharing in a dramatic exploration of a theme I can learn something about myself in the process, and quite another to suggest the drama is for me and about me. Yet we have trained generations of teachers who think drama is just this, that it is an expression of each child's ego, so that a bewildered teacher feels a responsibility not towards what is being created by a group of thirty, but towards thirty individual creations. Drama is not about self-expression. It is a group's expression, concerned with celebrating what people share, what man has in common with man. When an audience is responding to a play they are identifying what they have in common with the human beings on stage. Drama is about similarities not differences, but of course by looking at similarities, differences might well be highlighted.

Thus I claim that for decades we have attempted to change the nature of the art in order to meet the requirements of child-centred education – and have felt guilty because it does not work. I believe that Brian Way, a man of the theatre, also knows that child-centred drama in a pure form cannot work. He never actually says this in his publications, rather the reverse, but he offers a methodology that focuses away from the child. He creates a new set of skills, not the skills to do with refinement of speech that the Speech and Drama experts had a vested interest in, but *life-skills*. *Development through Drama* is a *training* manual.

2 The exercise mode

Influenced by Stanislavski (1937) in the theatre, Way has devised a parallel training for pupils in schools to help children develop, in particular, sensitivity, concentration and intuition. He believes that practice in, for instance, mirror exercises, would over a period of time develop these personal traits, so often neglected by a traditional curriculum. His book offers a wealth of pleasurable activities which have been seized upon by teachers as the 'five finger exercises' of creative drama. Apart from whether or not these exercises are effective (they are certainly found to be enjoyable and relaxing by many pupils), they have given the teacher a secure base from which to work, for the teacher can be very much in charge, dictating the choice of exercise, controlling the length of time for each, selecting the background music where felt to be appropriate or even dictating the moment-to-moment activity within the experience. As will be seen from the example below, the drama can be far removed from what could be recognised as a child-centred activity:

Continually there is value in the teacher telling the story whilst the class are doing it; everybody works at one and the same time, discovering for themselves how to do each thing. To start with, there is little detail in the story; as concentration and absorption grow with experience, the detail can increase by the teacher's approach and type of suggestion. For example, an early story (it is one of, shall we say, a visit to the sea-side) might start:

One morning you are fast asleep in bed. The alarm clock rings, so you get up and get washed; then you get dressed; then you have breakfast . . .'

. . . At a later stage, some detail begins to come in, and the start of the story might run:

'One morning you are fast asleep in bed; the alarm bell rings, so you push back the blankets and sheets, put on your slippers and go to the bathroom; then you wash your face and hands – and don't forget your neck and behind your ears . . .'

And at a later stage:

'So you go to the bathroom and turn the doorknob – push the door open – go inside – close the door gently behind you so that you don't wake up anybody else in the house; now you go to the basin – put the plug in – turn on the tap – it's a very stiff tap . . .' (p. 196).

The children are required to perform these actions as they hear the teacher's instructions. Not only does this teaching method put the teacher almost entirely in control, it also invites a particular kind of mental disposition from the participants. I have called this the 'exercise mode' of dramatic behaviour. In this particular instance it is representational, as the 'performance mode' is, for the child is required to *describe* in action whatever the teacher suggests (as in the example above, 'So you go to the bathroom and turn the doorknob'), but the 'exercise mode' has other characteristics that give it a special mental quality. They tend to be:

(*a*) it *isolates action* as being of interest in itself in a way that does not occur either in dramatic playing or performing. It also can isolate one action from another, so that the total sequence is not relevant (concentration on washing one's neck has little to do with the subsequent 'sea-side' actions – the action of washing one's neck is but an arbitrary item in a string of actions);

(b) it is inconsequential, removing any sense of import to do with an imagined situation;

(c) it is always short-term, so there is a strong sense of doing it in order to complete a task. This task orientation is not unlike the 'foreshadowing' mental set of the ideas game, not perhaps in the example of exercise quoted above, but in those kinds of exercises where you know the outcome before you start. (For example, 'you are going to ice a cake, carry it to a safe place – and trip over the cat!');

(d) sometimes there is a sense of doing it because it needs practising;

(e) if it requires a recall of emotion, it is often sufficient merely to switch on the emotion rather than elicit it (as when you trip over the cat!).

Although the quoted example of exercise happens to require a *describing* of appropriate actions, some exercises place the participant firmly in the 'dramatic playing' mode. For instance, 'You are going to try to persuade a friend to lend you some money' places the participant in the experiential frame, as the negotiation will *occur* and the outcome could take different forms. This still puts the participant in an 'exercise mode' as the dramatic playing that ensues is modified by the *task* orientation.

The 'exercise mode' can be very useful when the purpose is clear to both teacher and class. There are times when it is important to detach an action or an attitude in order to look at the mechanics of it. Unfortunately, some teachers, because of the obvious security it gives, give children a total diet of this kind of thing, which is a bit like English teachers giving children continual practice in punctuation or sentence structure without the chance to write creatively.

49

3 Widening of dramatic activities

One of the ways Brian Way has helped drama teachers is by broadening the repertoire of activities that might be included in a drama lesson. Like Dorothy Heathcote, he is interested in giving children an educational opportunity. He is not interested in drama as an important product in itself. It is surprising to what lengths he is prepared to go to ignore what is essentially drama. In the first paragraph of *Development through Drama* he writes:

> The Function of Drama
>
> The answer to many simple questions might take one of two forms – either that of information or else that of direct experience; the former answer belongs to the category of academic education, the latter to drama. For example, the question might be 'What is a blind person?' The reply could be 'A blind person is a person who cannot see'. Alternatively, the reply could be 'Close your eyes and, keeping them closed all the time, try to find your way out of this room'. The first answer contains concise and accurate information; the mind is possibly satisfied. But the second answer leads the inquirer to moments of direct experience, transcending mere knowledge, enriching the imagination, possibly touching the heart and soul as well as the mind. This, in over-simplified terms, is *the precise function of drama* [my italics] (p. 1).

In this paragraph we have the basis for Brian Way's philosophy: he is interested in introducing direct experience into education. This is not new in child-centred teaching, but Way extends the notion of direct experience to exercise of the senses in the way other theatre people like Rose Bruford (1958) have recommended for children. But whereas Rose Bruford's system of training is rigidly linked with conventional mime, Brian Way offers a much more flexible approach that anticipates much of the kind of sensitivity work of the encounter-group movement in the late 1960s. In the example above, so that children might imagine what it is like to be blind, the teacher invites them to deprive themselves temporarily of their sight. This is a fine example of direct experience – suddenly the pupils are thrown back onto their resources of space, memory and touch. This is direct experience, but *it is not drama* – not until there is some pretence involved, some symbolic representation, some intention to make believe. In which case moving around the room *with one's eyes open, as if* one could not see, would qualify for drama. Only in the most narrow sense is dramatic experience direct: one way of putting it is that drama is not itself direct, it only appears to be. That it appears to be is its power. Much teaching of drama has effectively removed that power. This is one of the paradoxes of the educational drama situation – that we have trained a generation of teachers who have not understood the nature of drama itself. They have not appreciated that Brian Way in advocating so many exercises in direct experience was desperately and effectively fighting a battle against second-hand learning which characterises so much of our traditional 'empty pitcher' view of education.

Thus Brian Way opened the door to all kinds of activities (games, relaxation exercises, 'warm-ups' and sensitivity exercises, etc.) to be done in the name of drama. The popular view expressed was that 'anything goes', because 'drama is life'. It took Chris Day (1975), writing eight years after Brian Way, boldly to affirm that, 'Drama . . . is not life' (p. 3).

I also suggest that much of the bewilderment felt by teachers about the nature of the subject that they were teaching can be traced to both Brian Way's and Dorothy Heathcote's disclaimer that drama could be important in itself. If it has so little status, why bother understanding it, one might ask!

Dorothy Heathcote

Because Dorothy is such a charismatic figure, many people thirst to see her on television or read about her.

Such people are going to be disappointed with what follows, for I shall merely continue to look critically at some of the concepts to which she has given prominence. I shall also attempt with Dorothy Heathcote, as I have with the other pioneers, to point to innovations or assumptions which are implicit in her work and which she herself may not have articulated. For it often happens that the things we take for granted are the very things that need most explaining, but to which we give least attention because we are barely conscious of them ourselves.

There is an outstanding example of this in Dorothy Heathcote, and that is her 'literary' assumptions about the content of drama. In this aspect she is linked, as I mentioned in Chapter One, with Harriet Finlay-Johnson who attached more importance to content than any pioneers since. For Harriet Finlay-Johnson, knowledge of the objective world was of prime importance and she developed a dramatic process of making factual knowledge more interesting. Whereas it would have been possible to ask Harriet Finlay-Johnson, 'What are you teaching this lesson?' and the answer could easily be something like, 'The Spanish Armada', one could not expect to be given an equivalent answer from Peter Slade, Brian Way or the Speech and Drama teachers. Now the content or subject-matter of any particular dramatic experience is for Dorothy Heathcote what gives it significance. But where she differs from Miss Finlay-Johnson is that she looks beyond the facts to more universal implications of any particular topic.

'I wonder why you keep going to sea when you know it's dangerous' (quoted by B. J. Wagner, 1976, p. 59), muses Mrs. Heathcote to a class of children who are into a drama about pirates – and she from then on carries at the back of her mind the possibility that through the subsequent experience these children might understand something of what drives people to face dangers. Now this is a *literary*, thematic way of looking at content. Just as a novel is about characters in a story sequence and at the same time, at a different level, about many other things, so drama has more than one level of meaning. And it is the thematic meanings, of course, that allow the participants to enter fantasy or unfamiliar contexts. It allows, to give another example, Tom Stabler's middle juniors to identify with the Bible story of Jezebel which at a surface level was quite outside their experience. The teacher's pre-planning ensures that the necessary connections are made. Tom Stabler describes the process in the Rosens' publication (1973):

> The children chose the theme of Jezebel, a foreign princess who introduces the worship of Baal to move the king towards selfish and evil acts. Elijah opposes, much as people's champion. Thus the theme offered clear-cut situations and opposing characters as a spring-board to varied developments and with the likelihood of the following abstract possibilities: duties of kingship; nature of law; and claims of a community, etc. (pp. 208–9).

Neither Dorothy Heathcote nor Tom Stabler, who had not done drama before he met Dorothy, appreciated that the above kind of thematic planning was in any way unusual. And yet as far as many practitioners were concerned it was revolutionary. Teachers who for years had planned in terms of appropriate *actions* could not overnight apply their minds to appropriate *meanings* as well. In my view this is one of the keys to understanding differences between Dorothy Heathcote and her predecessors in the field. But of course it requires a two-way thinking operation. It is not enough to be able to translate a topic into themes: ability to see a theme in turn translated back into action is a necessity. (It is sometimes amusing to watch an intellectually inclined teacher, happily aping what he or she thinks is a 'Heathcote-type' preliminary discussion, thrashing around helplessly incapable of finding a concrete start to the drama. Many postgraduates after three years of thinking in the abstract feel quite stupid when required to think concretely.)

But because Dorothy Heathcote has always taken the

importance of content for granted it has made her less than tolerant with dramatic activity that appears to lack significantly focused meaning. Tony Goode (1982) quotes this typically blunt Heathcote statement:

> A sort of messy, mucky drama has been going on for years, about unselectivity and conglomeration: 'Let them have the experience, all of them, every one of them, every minute of every time!' (p. 8).

And then Goode nicely juxtaposes this statement against one of Brian Way's:

> . . . if the approach is through the intellect rather than through intuition, that is, through a tangible and examinable process of understanding and thinking, rather than through an imaginative and emotional and therefore intangible process of relishing and enjoying, irrespective of whether or not there is full understanding (p. 8).

He says that the two quotations demonstrate where 'Way and Heathcote part company irrevocably' (p. 8), and he is right, but it is interesting to note that they both value intuition. I think Brian Way has in the past misjudged Dorothy Heathcote's work because he has seen it as intellectual. Indeed, my emphasis on her 'literary' conception of drama seems to confirm the view. On the other hand we have Wagner (1974) referring to her work as 'gut-level' drama. So there is an apparent contradiction here that could usefully be sorted out. Thinking thematically is in fact not necessarily an intellectual exercise. To think intellectually about pirates would be to categorise: 'Ah yes!' one might say, 'Drama about pirates could be about ships at sea or fighting or finding treasure or drinking rum, etc.' Now Dorothy's 'I wonder why you keep going to sea . . .' detaches itself from simple classification; its very phrasing has emotional overtones. Thus her thematic selections will always have a *feeling* quality. In other words she herself is opening up avenues for all sorts of intuitive meanings. Her thinking is already *person-*

alised: 'I wonder what keeps *you* going . . . etc.' And it is her intuition that she is dependent on for finding just the right thing to muse about to the class in front of her.

Likewise, she expects the children to operate intuitively in their make-believe, but she believes the intuition can be a refined instrument, accompanied by a high degree of awareness, at its best, bringing about reflection on what one experiences even as one experiences it. Absorption, so important to Peter Slade, is *not* a criterion for good quality endeavour. Hyper-awareness is what Dorothy Heathcote seeks. I shall be looking more closely at the implications of this point of view later, but here I want to suggest that in emphasising the importance of reflection Dorothy Heathcote has overstated the case. It seems to me, and we shall look at this in Chapter Seven when we examine the notion of unconscious learning in drama, that there is some truth in Brian Way's claim that relishing and enjoying something without fully understanding it can be of value.

There is, however, an even more fundamental division between their philosophies. When Brian Way speaks of direct experience 'transcending knowledge', he is denigrating knowledge in a way Dorothy Heathcote would never do. If he means by knowledge an accumulation of inconsequential facts then of course she would agree with him, but one suspects that in his concern for 'things of the heart' he is turning his back on the curiosity men share to know the world of objects. Now it seems to me that for Dorothy Heathcote man's curiosity about the world is the very source of her interest in drama, of her interest in history, of her interest in education and indeed, of her interest in Life. Early in Chapter One I referred to Marthinus' expression of regret that education persisted in training pupils to see a stone as a specimen and never for itself, to see the handler of a stone as a classifier of specimens and not as important in himself. Dorothy Heathcote would agree with Way and Marthinus that education as we currently understand it is too biased in this direction, but it is a balance between the two that she is seeking. Not, however, a balanced diet made up of a bit of one and then a bit of the other, but an integration between the two.

Now it is how Dorothy Heathcote sees the relationship between the two that sets her apart from most drama teachers. She is equally fascinated by the stone as a specimen and as a phenomenological object, but whereas those of us working in drama who might agree with the wisdom of this position tend to see 'personal engagement' with the world through dramatic action as a proper way of helping the child to know the world, Dorothy Heathcote tends to delay the phenomenological process by a deliberate depersonalising of objects. I have written elsewhere (Bolton, 1982) that the basic skill of acting is: 'an ability to engage with something outside oneself using an "as if" mental set to activate, sustain or intensify that engagement' and I go on to say, 'I am using the word "engagement" as a central feature because it implies a relationship at an affective level between a person and the world outside him' (p. 138). Now I am virtually claiming in this quotation that drama is about the 'personalising' of objects. For Dorothy Heathcote, whether the object is a shirt, a piece of leather, a chess-piece, a book or a surgeon's knife, the teacher's responsibility is to invite or even compel the children to work from a 'frame' (used here in the sociological sense of 'perspective') that requires not engagement, but *detachment*. Each child is to function as an 'expert' with all that implies of seeing the surgeon's knife as a specimen, as a tool, as a crafted artefact, as having a history of metal from the earth, of man's invention, of factory organisation, of training in high-quality skills.

This detachment does not and cannot remove affect. The scientist is motivated by a passion for what is true and a sense of responsibility towards what is true. Thus the affective is deeply embedded in everything a scientist does, but it is also a process of 'unselfing'. This is the kind of frame from which Dorothy Heathcote often (increasingly) wants children to work, and this is why it often seems to be the case in her work that the pupils are not *in role* at all – they are merely required to look at something from a particular scientific perspective.

But a 'drive towards truth' it might be argued, is surely an attitude the science teacher requires in the school laboratory. Is not this concentrated respect for the object as a specimen the very antithesis of the arts in education? Many of us indeed see the arts and sciences as pulling in different directions, 'different ways of knowing the world', we might say. But for Dorothy Heathcote, you can see the angels on the pin-head. Arts and sciences must be part of each other. By looking at the one you must see the other. Only by concentrating on the object can you both analyse it and celebrate it. Art and science are about how man makes sense of the world he lives in. Both centre on the object. The cobbler's song in *Hassan* is there because man invented a shoe. The material world is not only the source of man's arts, but the reason for them.

Thus the 'mantle of the expert' is always on the edge of society's rituals, myths, emblems, traditions, rejoicings and catastrophes. By examining the object the child earns the right to share the celebration of it. This is the key to Dorothy Heathcote's attitude to drama; may I suggest it is also a key to the re-thinking that will have to be done *vis-à-vis* the arts and the curriculum.

Thus there is a huge chasm between the two protagonists of this chapter. It is not surprising that practitioners and lecturers who have followed Brian Way's philosophy for all their professional lives feel very threatened. To them Heathcote does all the wrong things, says all the wrong things, and writes in the wrong way. She has no choice: she is burdened with both a philosophy and its implementation not conceived of by educators either in drama or in anything else. I can guess, for instance, that an academic in the drama field, Richard Courtney, was embarrassed by her in the early days because she does not fit his Sladian view of what drama teaching is about. Whereas he adopted caution, a long-time associate and friend of Brian Way, Margaret Faulkes Jendyk (1975), expressed her insecurity by writing the most vituperative article I have ever read by one educator of another. You cannot *not* react to Dorothy Heathcote. There is, however, always a danger that her critics are really writing about themselves, defending their own positions, so there has been very little constructive criticism. Even the medium of an academic thesis (1978) has been used by John Crompton, her colleague at Newcastle University, to express his scorn rather than offer a cool evaluation. There has also been a great deal of adulation which is perhaps even more harmful for it generates mysticism. Opportunity has now been presented for someone to take a sober look at her writings which have been collected into one volume recently by Liz Johnson and Cecily O'Neill (1983).

The next chapter will be rather different in both intention and structure, for it will not examine the work in detail of particular leaders in the field nor give attention to the teasing out of any particular principles. Rather, it attempts to give the reader a general picture of how other practitioners and commentators have responded to the various theoretical strands which the major pioneers have spun for us, and to demonstrate how the community drama movement, right up to the mid-1960s, uniquely outshone in both effort and prestige the work of pioneers in classroom drama.

Summary

In this chapter I have once more attempted to describe the work of two pioneers, while at the same time using their work as a platform for discussion of issues which are crucial to my own philosophy. In discussing Brian Way, I have suggested that not only has the emphasis placed by him on the individuality of the individual been misleading, it has also put some teachers in a position of distorting the medium of drama itself; and that Brian Way in practice overcame this problem by including in his seminal publication a system of *training* in life skills. He popularised the use of exercise, which, I have explained, dispositionally orientates the participants in a special way. I further suggested that he broadened the scope of the drama lesson by including all sorts of direct sense experiences. I argued that drama is not in itself direct, that indeed its power lies in its *seeming* directness.

Both Brian Way and Dorothy Heathcote believe in the importance of intuition, both for teacher and for pupil. Dorothy Heathcote's own thinking oscillates between the thematic and the concrete. This 'literary' slant to the drama's content is an important contrast with all previous pioneers, most of whom had given little attention to content. But more fundamental than this is her view of the scientist's and artist's conception of knowledge. According to her the material objects of the world provide the common source of that knowledge. Drama is but one way in which society makes sense of the material world. To know an object well is to earn the right to celebrate it.

4 Community theatre and other influences on drama in school

Although I suggested in the last chapter that it was easier for Brian Way than for Peter Slade to challenge the formal drama traditions within the schools, it could not be said that either of them had very much impact on what drama meant and still means to interested people outside our educational institutions. Innovators of 'informal' drama seem in fact to have failed abysmally in their attempt to explain their approach to the public at large and in particular to other subject teachers, headteachers and L.E.A. officials. A startling illustration of another educator's naive understanding of the work of drama teachers occurs in a recent publication by David Hargreaves (1982) who recommends that the arts and drama in particular should be given a place at the centre of the curriculum. But he writes:

> The number of drama teachers in schools has grown rapidly for years. But they are severely constrained by the time-table of forty-minute periods. School plays cannot be produced within such a framework. It is not surprising then that school plays ('theatre') must in practice be given a low priority. Most pupils' experience of drama must be confined to 'drama lessons' and the easiest way to conduct such a short lesson is to devote it to *improvised* drama and movement, with its focus on individual objectives. One of the central functions of drama is thereby distorted (p. 153).

In other words, he sees the informal activities of the drama lesson as a regrettable compromise falling far short of the main purpose of drama, the school play. It is something of a boost for drama teachers to have someone as eminent in education as David Hargreaves taking interest in the value of drama, but if the subject is to develop we must find ways of demonstrating its worth more effectively to more such 'outsiders'.

The lack of communication to others has only in part been due to our own ineptness at salesmanship; it more likely lies in a fairly deeply embedded resistance to drama being anything other than a community art – not just a performing art, a *community* art. David Griffiths, in a fascinating dissertation (1970), has documented its history. It is a history of morale boosting, of public money being made available from various sources from 1918 onwards: to enrich the life in remote villages in danger of being deserted by the exodus after the First World War; to occupy the unemployed in the 1930s on Tyneside; to counter the dreary effect of the 'blackout' during the Second World War (this was the first instance in this country of government subsidy); to bring a sense of well-being to the community during the difficult years following the war; and in particular, to occupy bored young people. It was this latter purpose which attracted most money, for in the 1940s and 1950s the government saw the development of youth clubs as one of its priorities. Drama, more than any of the other arts, became a popular pastime for young people which grew rapidly not just in quantity but also in standards, for the notion of *training* youth in drama seems to have been conceived from the beginning.

Now, by a quirk of history, the machinery for carrying out such schemes of training in drama was not to be found in normal educational administration, but in the huge network of social services administered by the National Council of Social Services, a voluntary body financed by Carnegie Trust which since 1919 had co-ordinated the work of various national organisations such as the Village Drama Society, County Rural Community Councils, British Drama League, the Federation of Women's Institutes, the National Association of Boys' Clubs, Townswomen's Guilds, the Workers' Educational Association, County Youth Committees, the Standing Conference of

Drama Associations and Hull University's Extra-Mural Department, the only university to take interest in Community Drama.

Thus when there was demand for training youth in drama the holder of the purse, the government, turned for advice not to educationalists, not to speech and drama experts (although there was some overlap here), but to a small group of charismatic figures who for decades had been promoting community drama of one sort or another, promoting it by giving advice, by running courses, by setting up drama libraries of play-texts, by making links with professional theatre, by popularising competitive festivals. These dynamic people, including Mary Kelly, Frances Mackenzie, L. du Garde Peach, Leo Baker, Robert Newton and Alfred Willett-Whittacker were not merely enthusiastic practitioners, they were far-sighted educators who were giving high status to amateur theatre. It is important for us to understand, therefore, that what was going on in schools in the 1920s, '30s, '40s and '50s paled into insignificance by the side of community drama.

As David Griffiths tells us, when, in the 1940s and 1950s it was necessary to make appointments to advise on Youth Drama in order to meet the requirements of the new Government project, these people were the experts, already familiar with training schemes, whose advice was sought. They were invited to recommend likely candidates for the newly-created posts of Drama Organiser to various counties who would oversee all adult dramatic activity including youth work. Many appointed in this way were ex-professional theatre actors or directors who for various reasons (not always the best) were interested in transferring to the amateur world. In 1949 the Drama Board was set up by Leo Baker as an examining body to give national qualification to tutors of youth drama. This represented a most enlightened step, which is perhaps even more remarkable when one appreciates that no educational institution was involved. The examination syllabus set new standards in the teaching of drama to young people and provided a spectacular contrast to the out-of-date, circumscribed speech and drama examinations of the Royal Academy, Guildhall and Trinity Colleges. But eventually Leo Baker, employed as Carnegie's full-time adviser, and certainly the most powerful leader in amateur theatre training in the country, gave way in the early 1960s to another younger yet just as skilful negotiator, Peter Husbands, who was finely in tune with the changing emphasis in the world of drama education. He persuaded the Board in 1970 to recognise that a new kind of qualification was now required, one that would give status to the more 'creative' approach to drama in schools. In many ways this innovation by Peter Husbands marks the watershed of drama education. Such was the respect in which the Drama Board was held by teachers, advisers and teacher-trainers alike that the profession as a whole gave support to this new examination, the first (apart from Peter Slade's own certificate in Birmingham) to give recognition to talented classroom teachers. (The sad demise of this Board in 1981 and the heartless handling of its distinguished Secretary, Peter Husbands, by the D.E.S. is a story that will have to be told elsewhere.)

When pressure was eventually put on L.E.A.s in the 1950s to take over employment of the various county organisers whose salaries hitherto had been paid from Carnhegie Trust funds, most authorities did so on condition that the organisers' work should be extended to schools. Thus began an era when larger-than-life 'theatrical' figures stalked the corridors of even our infant schools. Thus the 'real' drama scene of community theatre at last infiltrated the schools system. Speech and Drama teachers found themselves gaining unexpected support from 'the authority'.

It is not surprising that many Primary teachers at this time gave up trying their own hand at teaching the subject, leaving more and more to the 'expert'. The chance of drama becoming a tradition in our Primary schools has never been realistic. It took a new generation of drama advisers to attempt to bring it back again. A new breed of drama advisers, trained teachers, interested in the work of Slade and Way were appointed from the mid-1960s onwards. They inherited a suspicion or even a fear of drama often combined with the unspoken conviction shared by David Hargreaves that drama is a communal, performing art. Such convictions often remained unspoken for the pressure on teachers to move away from performance has been considerable. And of course in recent years there has been yet another pressure to move away from Brian Way's methods. Many of the latest appointees to influential positions are products of Dorothy Heathcote's and my own teaching. One wonders whether teachers are ever allowed to rest!

The message that teachers picked up most strongly from both Brian Way and Dorothy Heathcote was that the dramatic *process* was all important. Respect for product in the form of dramatic production became eroded and, regrettably, those who believed in the value of drama as a community enterprise gave up the struggle. School Drama Festivals, Youth Drama Festivals with notable exceptions almost disappeared (there must be a generation of young teachers coming into our profession who do not know what such things are) and even Adult Drama Festivals (probably for different reasons) became less popular. But in the 1980s we are in a new recession; morale is getting low, and soon the government will seriously turn to the arts as a 'booster'. There are already signs (I am actually writing this during the autumn of 1982) of a return to Community Arts. David Morton, Inspector for Drama in the City of Leeds and a deservedly respected figure among our Drama Advisers, writes in the latest publication on the Arts by the Calouste Gulbenkian Foundation (1982) of recent developments in Leeds. His initial reservations expressed here suggest that he, like many of us, has spanned an era of reaction against the worst excesses of cut-throat competitiveness and artificiality of performance in favour of the process of a child's personal experience. One can only admire his open-mindedness in allowing what would at first seem to him to be a reactionary step.

Origins

The Manager of the Grand Theatre, Leeds, went to see a school dance production, and was impressed by the quality of the work and offered his theatre to the educational establishments so that they would try to reach a wider audience. This worried me and other colleagues because, at that time, we felt that non-educational criteria were being imposed on school work and he was trying to fill his theatre at a slack time of the year. We were wrong – he had, and has, a real interest in the development of drama for learning, as well as drama for future audiences. This festival has developed from this. The following year saw the establishment of the Leeds Educational Drama Association. Its executive committee includes teachers, advisers, elected members of the City Council, and managers and directors of all the professional theatres in the city. The representation on this committee is deliberately political. It was felt that development of all aspects of drama would be best served by a composite body embracing education, local government and the professional theatre.

The festival now takes place in July at the Grand Theatre, the famous City Varieties, Leeds Playhouse, Leeds Civic Theatre, and three of the local authority's community theatres. In 1979 the festival embraced the National Festival of Youth Theatres when 14 Youth Theatre Groups from all over Britain joined the Leeds Festival and performed in the city's major theatres and participated in a week of workshop sessions led by national figures such as Henry Livings, Cicely Berry, Willie Hobbs, Sue Little and others. In 1981, 56 groups participated, including four who will offer street theatre in shopping precincts in the centre of town. 3,000 youngsters, approximately, will participate and audiences are likely to run at around 15,000, most of whom will be young people.

Why a Festival?

The reason for the festival remains as originally envisaged by the Manager of the Grand Theatre, that is, to provide a showcase to a wider audience of the type of performance work that can be seen in schools and Youth Theatre Groups. The work varies from established to original (improvisation-based) pieces, from opera, rock shows and musicals, to anthology (art, poetry, dance, text, improvisation) programmes from primary and middle schools. Through this we aim to develop and heighten the drama experience of youngsters within the education service, to link the curriculum work with performance in a professional theatre and the experience which this brings to youngsters, and for groups to share their work with others, often from different backgrounds and cultures.

Achievements

These are difficult to assess. As a public relations exercise the festival is clearly a success and is now an official part of the civic calendar. The youngsters clearly learn much from working with professionals in professional theatres and in workshops with tutors from the professional theatre. However, one still feels that the processes of preparation within the schools and youth theatre groups are the most valuable learning areas, yet, these areas must be heightened by the youngsters' realisation that they will eventually perform in a well-equipped, professional space.

In conclusion

Many people have reservations about festivals of drama for young people, even of non-competitive ones such as this in Leeds. At one stage I had the same reservations, but in the light of the experience of the last six years and the credibility that the festival has given to drama with elected members, headteachers, and officers of the Authority, I am convinced that, at any rate for Leeds, this annual festival is helping to develop the quality of drama in the Authority (pp. 44–45).

I think the above account speaks for itself. It points the way to new directions for the late 1980s and 1990s.

But to return to our historical account, as if the picture was not already complicated enough, the Ministry of Education found its own way of promoting drama – to align it with Physical Education, a policy which was gradually put forward by certain Inspectors for Physical Education over a period of 20 years from about 1945. (It should be noted, however, that the Staff Inspector with special responsibility for drama, Mr. A. F. Alington, held a more eclectic view as his manual on teaching drama (1961), published some time after his retirement, reveals.) In 1949 H.M.S.O. published an unusual document, *A Story of a School*, which was an account of movement-centred education advocated by a Birmingham head-master, Peter Stone, who was to become one of the West Riding's Physical Education Organisers. His work with children was an adaptation of Laban's principles of movement which became known in this country during the war. It had the advantage of not only offering a system of training (that it was intended by Rudolf Laban for the re-training of ballet dancers did not deter physical educationalists from transferring it to colleges and schools), but also of offering a rationale. A theory was evolved by a few influential educationalists that if a child is given a basic training in Laban skills then he will have the essential grounding for any future specialisation he may care to follow in gymnastics, dance or drama.

Now H.M.I.s with considerable influence, particularly Ruth Foster (Staff Inspector for Women's Physical Education and, significantly, Chairman of the Inspectorate's Drama Panel) and Jim Gill (Staff Inspector for Teacher-Training) took Peter Stone to their bosom, so to speak, and Drama-through-Movement became the official Ministry and then D.E.S. doctrine, and a view was subsequently promoted that a child could not do drama until he first learnt to express himself through movement. (So in some schools keen on the creative arts, children never opened their mouths in drama lessons!) Let me hasten to say that in many schools, particularly in the West Riding, fine education took place, but far from it helping to increase drama in schools, it had the reverse effect for two reasons: (1) it appeared once more to be something that could only be handled by a specialist – this time a P.E. specialist, and (2) the conceptual relationship between movement and drama had never been worked out sufficiently for the practical relationship to become clear. Another curious historical twist to the story is that whereas women teacher-trainers in P.E. welcomed Laban movement, their male counterparts virtually said, 'Over our dead bodies!' So a Primary school headmaster, for instance, could find his school offering movement experience to children who had female teachers to the neglect of those children who were unfortunate enough to have a man as their teacher, and similarly, Movement and Drama appeared as a subject on the time-table in our Secondary schools where there happened to be a woman in the P.E. department who was interested. One way or another, drama got left out in the cold.

Fortunately, at a time when this 'established' D.E.S. view of drama was at its peak in the early 1960s, a newcomer appeared among the group of Physical Education biased Inspectors. John Allen, a man experienced in straight theatre, children's theatre and radio, who, although deeply impressed by the high quality of movement teaching both in the regular D.E.S. courses for teachers and in schools, nevertheless sought to erode the 'official' image by bringing entirely new faces into the D.E.S. courses. Thus teachers, advisers and college lecturers had the chance to work with personalities as varied as Colette King, Keith Johnstone, Philip Hedley, Peter James and Robert Witkin.

John Allen became the most well-informed person in the country about what was going on, for the new Minister of the Arts, Jenny Lee, invited him to survey drama in schools and colleges. His *Education Survey 2 Drama* (1967), totally lacking in officialese, lucidly, wittily reports on a rag-bag of activities done in the name of drama and with an almost total lack of rationale behind the subject. He confirms people's fears when he writes:

> It has been surprising, nevertheless, to find how much time is being devoted in schools and colleges to a subject of whose real identity there is no general agreement (p. 2).

John Allen was respected by leaders in all walks of drama education and theatre and consequently was able to give a great deal of energy to getting opposing groups to talk to each other, so that, for instance, in 1970, he was responsible for bringing teacher-trainers in drama and drama advisers together at a conference in Exeter. As David Griffiths (1970) points out, these two élite factions had not met since the notorious Bonnington Conference in 1948 when war between two views of drama educators was openly declared. In a letter to David Griffiths for his dissertation, Mary Robson, a retired Head of Drama at Neville's Cross College of Education, recalls the division at the Bonnington Conference eloquently:

> After more than twenty years, when details have faded, my main impression of the Bonnington Conference remains the same – the conference of the sheep and the goats, very firmly divided the central aisle of the hall, Drama Organisers on one side, Training College lecturers on the other. I remember the shock of realising that the two groups were not making any contact – the word DRAMA meant entirely different things to each side. I had a distinct impression that many of the organisers had had professional theatre experience and that, naturally, their point of view was coloured by this, while the teachers had arrived at the point of realising the potential of drama as a tool of education. The only person on the organisers' side of

the room who spoke a language I understand, was Peter Slade, a trim, slight figure, quietly expounding his belief in the value of drama in work with children. He seemed to cause embarrassment to his side of the room, but a sense of doors opening and light coming in to mine (p. 41).

It is not recorded whether there were H.M.Is present at the Bonnington Conference. Thanks to John Allen and the respective chairmen of the two groups, Brian Watkins (ATCDE Drama Section) and Ray Moss (National Association of Drama Advisers), the Exeter Conference set up a dialogue between lecturers and advisers which has continued in the regions ever since. Indeed, many share the running of Drama Board (transferred to the Royal Society of Arts from 1981) courses.

The Schools Council

When the Drama sub-committees of the Schools Council English Panel were presented with a proposition from Lynn McGregor, a London teacher with a strong interest in the sociology of education and her own research into Drama teaching on its way (1976), to launch a full-scale research project, the climate seemed ripe for the sub-committee to make a recommendation. The result was a three-year project conducted by Lynn McGregor, Maggie Tate and Ken Robinson which culminated in a major publication (1977) and an excellent film of dynamic teaching (*Take Three*). The project was most ably supervised by the Schools Council Curriculum Officer, Maurice Plaskow. A much more modestly financed project was subsequently initiated to look at Primary School Drama (1979) under the directorship of Tom Stabler.

For the first time a fairly extensive observation exercise was initiated involving close reporting of the drama teaching in six education authorities conducted throughout the period of one academic year. One quite serious limitation in the original selection of these authorities lay in the criterion for selection which seemed to rest in the main on those authorities whose drama advisers happened to be currently in favour with H.M.I. This tended to give a certain bias to the work likely to be found in schools, especially as the coterie of advisers who knew each other's work well, often teaching on each other's courses and jointly helping to tutor the national D.E.S. courses in turn, tended to select for observation those schools where they had a good relationship with the drama specialist. It would have been interesting, and perhaps fairer, to have looked at the drama work in an authority either where no drama adviser existed or where he or she did not have the accolade of inspectorial approval. Presumably none of the former volunteered for the project!

What they did achieve in terms of breadth was a nice balance among kinds of schools, geographical positions and rural/inner city contrasts. Altogether 159 lessons were observed by the team. Sadly one has to conclude, if the illustrations of lessons reported in the published text are anything to go by (and one can hardly conceive that the team held back good lessons) then we still have a long way to go before we can claim with confidence that drama on the curriculum guarantees good education. The observers met some very good teachers who were working in very unsympathetic conditions within a school, and other teachers who were muddled in their thinking about aims, and yet others who did not know how to bring any educational or artistic guts to the drama lesson. These things, not surprisingly, are only hinted at in their publication, for that document is mostly concerned with presenting the reader with the team's own rationale. Nevertheless, I believe that in its veiled way, the report is a very proper indictment of the drama scene – as it was perceived by these three sharp young people in 1974–75.

Where does the fault lie? We can blame the schools for not providing the right conditions, we can blame the government and local education authorities for not giving sufficient attention to in-service training, but I think the buck must rest with people like me who had by that date been employed in teacher-training for just over ten years. We simply had not evolved a theory and practice of teacher-training that works. Very recently David Davis (1982) has made a scholarly contribution to this field and has been fortunate enough to have the chance to put theory into practice at Birmingham Polytechnic where under the leadership of Brian Watkins a specialist course of considerable merit and vision for P.G.C.E. students has been introduced. But this is still a rare instance, Likewise, at the in-service level, very few authorities can match the well-conceived programme of courses for teachers produced over a number of years by Geoffrey Hodson and Maureen Price of I.L.E.A. But until we can sort out our muddled thinking that surrounds the subject, there is a danger that the next 'official' report will not fare any better. No doubt the first four chapters of this book, in attempting to describe the confusion, are also managing to add to it! Let us hope that later chapters clear away some of the murkiness. In the meantime let us continue to look at the Schools Council Report.

Most writers on education tend to be people well-established in the profession. Here in *Learning through Drama* we have a group of three people whose years of teaching combined did not add up to more than twenty. This is but one way of reminding ourselves what an extraordinarily good job they did of the 'conceptual framework', as they called it. I do not think it can be claimed that they opened up new territory (writings by Dorothy Heathcote and others in the 1970s were concerned with a level of sophistication in drama teaching which the team seemed not to be able to articulate), but in terms of giving some sense of order to the basic functioning of drama the publication deserves to be seen as an important landmark. The very title, *Learning through Drama*, pointed many teachers who had seen drama merely as a diversion offered in the name of self-awareness in a more positive direction. It attempted to identify the components of learning with a clarity not found elsewhere. Indeed, the team was so anxious to give recognition at last to the importance of the *content* of any particular drama, that it seems almost to be reinforcing the dualistic assumption that drama is about attitudes or ideas in the children's heads to be explored and then expressed through the medium. This further seemed to give encouragement in practice to the 'go-into-groups-discuss-an-important-issue-and-find-a-dramatic-state-ment-for-us-to-discuss' sequence. Indeed, the term 'dramatic statement', to which they become quite attached as the book proceeds, perhaps takes us too firmly in the direction of propositional knowledge translated into dramatic coding. It is not the authors' intention to give it this gloss. They assure us:

> In a strict sense it is not so much the content of drama which is distinctive, but the way in which it is considered (p. 16).

Nevertheless, John Allen (1979) is right to summarise the overall impression thus:

> If it is weak on aesthetics, it is notably strong on pedagogy, almost to the extent of limiting the concept of learning (p. 80).

Weak on aesthetics it undoubtedly is, and yet curiously it is the only book on drama in education lucky enough to find its way into the impressive bibliography of the 1982 Calouste Gulbenkian publication on the Arts in Schools. What started out as an intention by the authors of *Learning through Drama* to express 'a specific point of view' (p. 8) has apparently become the only authoritative reference!

Other Trends

This section will be a brief summary of other influences which have left their mark on the drama education scene. One of the most popular trends has been that of Drama

Games. These seem to come from two kinds of sources; either the Theatre Games of Viola Spolin (1963) or an extension of the widening of activities in drama lessons introduced by Brian Way. Sue Jennings' (1973) approach to Drama Therapy is a good example of all sorts of group and individual game-like experiences being referred to as drama. Ed Berman, a naturalised British citizen originally from America, over a number of years has set up courses for teachers in the use of games. So popular was this usage at one time that I recall examining final school-practice for one college when in observing two full days of drama lessons I only saw games, no drama at all. Clive Barker (1977) of Warwick University has given new substance to the use of games in the training of actors and Brian Watkins (1981) has evolved a theoretical framework conceptually linking drama and game in a way which I shall attempt to build on in the next chapter. Another American, Donna Brandes (1979 and 1981) has an approach to drama games based on Gestalt Therapy.

The purpose of these games has been in the main to do with releasing energy and reducing inhibitions or achieving group cohesion. Another form of game which has become popular among teachers other than drama teachers has been 'simulation', where elaborate game structures are set up usually involving a great deal of time and application in order to teach some specific subject-matter about the civic planning of motorways, starvation in the Third World or executive decision-making in industry. One of the earliest publications on this kind of work is by John Taylor and Rex Walford (1972). Many drama teachers have devised their own versions of this method. Dorothy Heathcote, in working with Gas Board executives, typically worked through analogy rather than simulation.

One of the important trends in recent years initiated in this country by John Hodgson (1972, 1973, 1975) has been for a number of drama specialists to undertake an editorial role in an attempt to raise the standard of literature on our subject. Ken Robinson, too, has successfully taken on the role of one-man interpreter, friend, challenger, articulator and spokesman not only for drama but for the arts in education generally (1980 and 1982). We are grateful to Ken Byron for setting up a much needed journal in Drama and Dance Education. A great hole had certainly been left by the demise of John Hodgson's series on *Drama in Education* and by *Young Drama*.

Other recent developments have pointed to changes of philosophy. There is a continuous passionate cry from Malcolm Ross in Exeter University to bring drama back to the Arts fold, a 'come-home-and-all-will-be-forgiven' gesture. A contrary pull may be observed in the polemics of some T.I.E. groups and a number of London based teachers who want a more honest appraisal of drama education as a political tool. Combining therapy and politics in an interesting way that still has to reach this country is the work of Bjorn Magner (1972) who, in Sweden, has used a kind of political psychodrama, not in order to point out weakness in our society but to refine each individual's capacity for political awareness.

There are signs of growth, but in case there is a danger of too much optimism, let me remind the reader that as recently as 1978 the Department of Education and Science published a document entitled *Primary Education in England* in which drama was not mentioned.

5   The 'game' of drama

I have taken the title of this chapter from a Durham University M.Ed. thesis by Geoff Readman (1984). The literal and metaphorical juxtaposition of drama and game is what I want to explore here. I am also grateful to Brian Watkins who was the first to put the idea to me that drama is a game. Much of what I write here will be based on his writings, particularly his book, *Drama and Education* (1981). It seems to me his basic analogy is a useful one and well worth expanding – I hope he approves of my attempt to do so!

The first known liturgical drama in England is *Quem Quaeritis?* (Goldman, 1975). As priests and choir chant the story of the resurrection one priest is instructed to move away *as if* from the tomb, and then to turn back when another sings in Latin 'Whither goest thou?' Thus in a simple action the past tense of narrative is transformed into the present and the *presence* of drama. The celebrants are brought into a new relationship with the substance of their celebration. It is a shared ritual quickened by dramatic action.

This illustration serves to show both what is distinctly dramatic and the kinship of drama to corporate celebration. Drama is at one with the rituals, the pageants, the festivals and the processions and all the forms with which men and women celebrate. But its uniqueness, its disturbing habit of making immediate and concrete things which are best revered from a distance has laid it open to charges of 'magic' or 'blasphemy' or 'sacrilege' or 'obscenity'. Western society has generated a deep suspicion from which in the main the other arts have been protected. As Jonah Barish (1969) has pointed out, embedded in our language is a common usage of artistic metaphors of which the dramatic ones are unambiguously pejorative. He cites 'melodramatic', 'stagey', 'theatrical', 'play-acting', 'putting on an act', 'putting on a performance', 'making a scene', 'making a spectacle of oneself', 'playing to the gallery', and compares the implied hostility of such expressions with the more approving tones of terms derived from the other arts: 'harmonious', 'symmetrical', 'graphic', 'shapely', 'well-balanced', 'poetic', 'in accord', 'in unison', 'in concert', 'chime in with', 'in tune with'.

The mediaeval church was divided on the issue of whether there was impropriety in the mimetic representation of holy personages on stage. One eleventh-century Latin drama, Rouen Pastores, avoided the problem by having a cut-out figure of the Virgin Mary in the midst of the stable scene, other parts being played by real people. Although disapproval of sacred dramas continued to be vehemently expressed, as, for instance, by Gerhoh of Reichersburg (1039–1169) who, according to Kolve (1966), warned that he who portrays the rage of Herod is guilty of the very vice he portrays (a deep-seated objection not entirely eradicated today), anxiety about its blasphemous nature was dispelled as more people came to regard it as merely a 'game' rather than as a sacriligious act. Language usage contributed to this slackening of clerical resistance. For the dramas were given the generic term of *ludus* (play) which carried overtones of pastime, merriment and revelling. And the actors 'played'; they did not act or perform; they did not, as we would say today, 'stage' a performance of the Passion; but rather, they *played the game of the Passion*.

As Kolve argues, '"Game" usages are crucial to an understanding of the mediaeval conception of drama' (pp. 14–15). Play and game are used interchangeably – it does not matter which. But what does matter is that relegation of drama to the same order of non-seriousness as game, revellings and disportings, permitted an 'it's only a game' attitude – both dismissive and tolerant – to creep in. To the mediaeval mind, 'game' stood in antithesis to 'earnestness', and so what took place on the pageant cart could be equated with other street pastimes.

An ambivalence, however, persisted. The magic of the drama game with its ambiguous morality and propriety remained as part of its fascination. The devil on stage might just *be* the Devil. Kolve refers to a sixteenth-century story about a player from a pageant wearing his devil's costume while going home, 'frightening everyone grievously'. Today very young children at a puppet show or a pantomime may have to be reassured that 'it is not real'. Many T.I.E. teams know what it is like to play in a school for educationally sub-normal children who cannot (or do not want to) distinguish between the 'baddy' character and the actor – who finds himself molested as he retreats to his car after the show!

But the conventions surrounding the drama itself usually go some way to counter this kind of misapprehension even in mediaeval times. Kolve describes the formalities of the Corpus Christi performance:

> Formal and repetitive in nature, it played year after year within a specifically limited time and place. Within those limits special conventions applied, creating a temporary world within the world of real life, and dedicating this created world to the performance of an act somewhat gratuitous to urgent daily concerns. Once this conventional world had been established, it was easily recreated until it became traditional. Like all play, this drama depended on formal order, without which progress within a game and pleasure from a game are alike impossible: anyone who breaks the rules spoils the game, makes it a poor and foolish thing (p. 20).

In emphasising form and the 'gratuitousness' to daily concerns Kolve is reflecting the writing of the Dutch anthropologist and philosopher Johan Huizinga (1970) who also sees play (in all its senses) as something apart from 'ordinary life' and as a means of 'creating order'.

In the above discussion the terms play and game have become interchangeable. I would like to suggest that all activities that take us outside the practical business of living (sacred worship, carnivals, listening to music and reading a novel, etc., etc.) can be seen as either subsumed under play or as extensions of it. The constraints, pressures, stresses, necessities and obligations of life are temporarily held in abeyance and we allow this 'second order' of experiencing to take over. As Huizinga puts it, for *Homo Ludens*, it is 'non-serious and yet intensely absorbing'. It is a kind of bracketing-off from everyday events. As we shall explore in the next chapter, it can be an experience that is both liberating and protecting.

Many writers interested in these phenomena tend to specialise either in child play or in the arts, the former finding clues in the activity which relate to child development, the latter establishing art as an enhancement of what is good and beautiful. Narrowing the field to either one or the other of these, has sometimes trapped the theoreticians into claiming that they have identified a defining characteristic of their field. For instance, Arnaud Reid (1982), in arguing that what all the variety of art forms have in common is the requirement of 'aesthetic intention', explains:

> For – cutting straight through the recurring controversies about whether, because of the varieties of the arts and of the infinity of differences between different individual works, 'art' can be 'defined' – one thing, I think, is clear. There is something common to all our experiences of art, of whatever kind – music, poetry, painting . . ., each art concretely utterly different from the others. It is that any work of art, of whatever kind or *genre*, must be experienced 'aesthetically'. What is called the 'aesthetic attitude' or interest in an object, is sometimes described as 'disinterested interest'. This is intended to mean that the object is attended to, and in some sense 'enjoyed' 'for itself', 'for its own sake', for the qualities it possesses in itself as apprehended, and which arouse our attention and interest (p. 4).

Now I would like to suggest 'disinterested interest',

enjoying something for its own sake, is a defining characteristic of all 'second order' experiencing, whether it is writing a poem, playing football, telling a joke or making a model aeroplane.

In a sense 'play' can become the generic term for all these varieties of activity on the basis of 'disinterest'. And, by implication, they all fulfil the mediaeval conception of non-seriousness. But this notion – that one set of activities is serious and therefore by implication another set *must* be non-serious – is a naive view, for it presupposes that first and second order experiences operate within the same frame and are therefore amenable to comparison. As Bateson (1973) argues, the psychological frame appropriate in discussing play or games is more akin to a picture frame than to the logical frame of a mathematical set: what is outside the picture frame is irrelevant and one can only make judgements of comparison and contrast on matters within the frame. One cannot say, for instance, that the artist's portrait is serious but the wallpaper on which the picture hangs is not, or vice versa. By this token serious/non-serious and even true/false are irrelevant dimensions.

To digress for a moment, that the apparent non-seriousness of play is a paradox is something which many anti-progressive educationists have chosen to ignore. It suits the purpose of, for example, R. F. Dearden (1976), Professor of Education at Birmingham University, to assume the naive view of non-seriousness and therefore to argue that for this reason even Wendy House play in the Infant School could not possibly be taken seriously as a medium for learning. Dearden was, of course, joining the ranks of Professors Peters and Hirst in their misguided pursuit of spelling out the logic of education and overlooking its dynamics in doing so.

What such educationists fail to recognise is the high degree of concentration and attention that all kinds of play evokes. It is a pity that, instead of dismissing it as non-serious, they have not devoted their knowledge and experience to exploring ways in which we might more effectively (and granted there is plenty of evidence of bad education carried out in the name of free play) harness this natural power for learning. It is my view that our 'establishment figures' in education have held back progress for a generation. Equally foolish in my view, to return to the central subject of this book, is the insistence by Brian Way that children should be given practice in concentration, for second-order activities are nothing if not absorbing. Some researchers, Sarah Smilanski in particular (1968), have attempted to show that some underprivileged children cannot engage in play, but lack of concentration is a sympton not a cause. Indeed, some privileged adults cannot play, but concentration is not the problem!

One of the reasons why play is so absorbing is that it is self-initiated, in a way that is not available to us in the process of combatting, enduring or avoiding the slings and arrows of day-to-day living. Paradoxically it provides this sense of freedom to choose, but the process of play activity is about *limiting* the choices. (It is interesting that Piaget failed to recognise what Vygotsky (1933, tr. 1976) observed about a young child's play: that it is rule-bound.) In a game the rules are socially constructed beforehand; in creative drama they are negotiated, but this negotiation is often constrained by whatever the 'rules' happen to be in the slice of life the creative drama is reflecting.

I now want to suggest that play, games and drama have the same structural basis, that in bringing a sense of order to the randomness of day-to-day living, they nevertheless build on structures embedded in our real social interactions. It is not surprising that in recent years they have served interchangeably in the hands of various theorists as models of each other. Sutton-Smith (1971) uses the game model to describe play. Erving Goffman (1969) and Rom Harré (1979) have used the dramatic model to describe social interaction. Michael Argyle et al. (1981) have employed the game model to do the same. Brian Watkins and Lawrence Stenhouse (1981) have used the game model to describe drama. Both Argyle and Watkins in using the game model have to play down the competitiveness of games, for neither the social interactions of real life nor of drama are necessarily competitive. But having made that reservation I would like to press the analogy between drama and game even closer. The apparently quaint mediaeval notion of 'playing the game of the Passion', I want to suggest, brings us nearer both to the way Caldwell Cook approached scripted work with his pupils and (more relevant to what will be discussed in the rest of this chapter) to classroom drama. Creative drama and game are structurally and anthropologically very close. What follows is an examination of structure and of how an awareness by the teacher of its significance can help him find the game in the drama.

Drama structures

For the above sub-heading I have deliberately copied from the title of a recent publication by Cecily O'Neill and Alan Lambert (1982), for it is a manual offering guidance to teachers in their planning of projects for drama. Central to the planning are not clearly defined objectives but clearly defined structures. The main strength of the book lies in the fact that most of their lesson material is from actual classroom practice. I shall from time to time use some of their material for further analysis and in order to make clear what I mean by structure.

The kind of structure the authors mostly discuss is to do with how to move from one dramatic experience into another in a way that tightens the pupils' grip on the central issue. For instance, in a drama project on 'The Way West' (p. 36) with a class of first-year secondary pupils, the lesson begins with the following sequence:

(1) The teacher shows a genuine photograph of a group of people who travelled together on the Oregon trail.
(2) She holds a discussion on why people might choose to undertake the dangerous journey.
(3) In pairs one partner assumes the role of any one of

the people in the photograph and tells the other (a colleague, friend or relative) why he is tempted to go on the journey.

(4) Class together again – the second partners report to the rest of the class what they have heard.

(5) Teacher-in-role starts a class improvisation as if they were a local community in the mid-west hearing what a bright future they might have if only they would abandon their homes and move west.

Now here we have a typical example of teacher-structuring when the topic is not one with which the children are familiar. The teacher is faced with the persistent problem of how to help children feel the action has started when the truth is they do not have either enough factual or empathetic resources to identify with the historical situation.

Now there is a *structural sequence* here that reveals thoughtful planning. Features of this sequence are brevity and variety. Too long a time with any one of the above steps of the sequence would only serve to emphasise their ignorance, whereas variety offers opportunity for different kinds of engagement. We can summarise the steps as follows:

(1) Picture $\longrightarrow$ (2) Discussion $\longrightarrow$ (3) Exercise $\longrightarrow$

(4) Reporting $\longrightarrow$ (5) Class improvisation

This is an admirably built sequential structure because although each short sequence is outwardly different, the emotional and thematic centre remains the same. Each step is but a different way of helping the class to begin to internalise the gravity of a family's decision to face unknown dangers. The concept is an enormous one for twelve-year-olds to grasp with any sense of reality, for many children of that age would regard it as fun if their family had to go away to new lands – just as I can recall at that age receiving the news of the outbreak of the Second World War with great joy! The teacher of 'The Way West' knows it is going to take perhaps several lessons before they really understand, from an adult point of view, what responsibility such a decision entails. In the meantime the drama has to start and to start simply.

Further analysis of the above five steps could be conducted (for instance, it is worth noting that they are made up of (1) non-drama → (2) non-drama → (3) drama → (4) non-drama → (5) drama activities) but it is not in the matter of graded steps within a sequence that drama resembles a game: the game element of drama is inherent *within each step*. Each of the 'drama steps' is a separate game. What I want to examine in detail is how the *interactional structure* of any particular dramatic episode provides the dynamics of a game experience.

In the five steps above there were only two that were dramatic – where one partner had to speak in role and the class improvised. Now if we look at the first of these in terms of structure we can see that it can be defined as a dramatic *exercise*, fulfilling the principal requisite of exercise as outlined in Chapter Three – a commitment to a short-term *task*. It is a useful first example for us to look at for it seems so simple – and yet even in something as straightforward as this, the structure can be adjusted in quite a sophisticated way.

Let us start the analysis. It requires a talker and a listener. There is a 'slackness' about such an active/passive relationship. For the listener, there is nothing to keep her to this role unless she happens to have a partner whose talk is engaging (or, of course, there may be extrinsic pressures of, for example, wanting to please teacher, which because it is always a possible element in children's work I will not keep referring to but will take for granted). The *interactional* structure for the talker requires a sustaining of partner's attention. The *psychological* structure for the talker requires, broadly speaking, two kinds of pretence: (1) an emotional one of having made a momentous decision and (2) a fictitious factual background.

It is the *interactional* structure that I am most interested in in this chapter, but, as we shall see, the psychological and interactional structures are mutually dependent. So in this particular dramatic exercise the interactional structure could be described as 'one player sustaining the attention of another player'. But the teacher of this lesson wisely does not want it left as 'slack' as that: she qualified the listener's contribution by suggesting she should be in role as a friend, colleague or relation. Now this not only affects the psychological structure for the listener, it more pertinently affects the dynamics of the interaction. For the focus of the interchange has narrowed so that the talker's role can *demand* the attention of the listener's role. Indeed as friend, colleague or relation, the listener has a choice of responses which were not available to her had the task merely instructed her to listen: she could, for instance, adopt a cool intellectual probing, helping the talker to weigh up the pros and cons, or she could set up emotional resistance to the idea. Notice the teacher did not add any further instructions for the listener. Had she for instance dictated that the partner should offer resistance this would have been a relatively crude way of 'tightening' the structure compared with instrucing the listener to be in a 'counsellor' role. On the other hand, the teacher could have injected an element extrinsic to the drama in the structure by warning the listeners beforehand that they were going to be required to make an accurate report to the rest of the class with the talkers assessing their report for accuracy. The choices for structure can be summarised as follows:

(1) Basic Structure – one person engaging another.
(2) Teacher dictates role for listener as friend, etc. but does not specify attitude.
(3) Crude resistance to idea from listener.
(4) Sophisticated, neutral questioning by listener.
(5) Teacher warns beforehand that the reporting back has to be accurate (extrinsic).

This teacher chose not to offer a tight structure to the class. In choosing (2) she would realise that some pupils would be virtually at (1) for some listeners would not take advantage of the 'role' opportunity. This is of course very useful diagnostically where the teacher does not know the class. How the different pairs respond will indicate to her whether any of them are mature enough in drama to structure for themselves. If she is lucky she may find that at least a few children appreciate that (4) makes for a better drama game than (3), and that (1) is so bland that it doesn't feel like a game at all! In some circumstances, however, a teacher would be foolish to risk leaving it at (2); it may well be necessary to adopt (3) as an instruction to the class as the only way of engaging their interest. It is not just children who may be incapable of operating their own structuring within an exercise. Sometimes adults, inexperienced and suspicious of drama, could not cope with a vague suggestion that the second partner should be in role as a friend, colleague or relative. It may be absolutely necessary to spell out the sophisticated potential of (4), the counselling role, for their resistance to doing drama may well block them from making connections between what seems a puerile exercise and anything of significance to themselves. So the teacher has to make the connections for them initially. And further extrinsic tightening of the structure may be appropriate – the teacher announces beforehand (this is an adult equivalent of (5)) that the talkers are to give an assessment of their partners as counsellors when the exercise is over.

I hope I have made it clear now that although (1) to (5) are basically the same structure, each modification is itself a sufficient change to make it a different kind of game – and thus the *experience* is a different one according to which is chosen (either by the teacher or the participants themselves). If as reader, you cannot imagine how different they are in structure I suggest you try your hand at *drawing* the relationship between the partners for each example. Structure is a relationship between two elements within a context, and graphics can often show that relationship more clearly than words.

Our starting point for analysing structure happens to have been with an exercise, the form of drama popularised by Brian Way, and yet little attempt has so far been made by him or by anyone else to show how these apparently slight adjustments within the structure of the exercise can seriously affect the outcome. With so much emphasis these days on using role-play with adolescents for Life Skills we need to train our teachers to be sensitive to the meaning and usage of structure.

But it is not the exercise mode that interests me the most. I think, as I have said elsewhere, exercise is a useful device but no more than that. There has been an advantage in looking first at an exercise because its very 'task' orientation often makes the structure explicit, whereas in group drama one has often to look for it. Indeed I shall be arguing that the drama will only be effective when its inner structure is felt by the participants. If it is to be *felt* by the participants then it is not too much to suggest that it should be *understood* by the teacher. Let us therefore look at the only example of group improvisation in the five steps outlined by the 'Way West' project. I will quote the full description.

The Meeting
The class are sitting in a circle. The teacher asks them to imagine that they are in a meeting place in a small town in the Mid-West. Perhaps it is a school-room, or a church hall. She explains that she will be taking part in the next activity.

She introduces herself as a representative of the government. She has come to tell them about the opportunities which await them if they are prepared to make the long journey to Oregon. The government will give them free farming land and the country is extremely fertile. They will be much more prosperous if they decide to move.

She encourages the class to ask questions about Oregon, and the kind of journey they will have to undertake to get there. Questions focus on such subjects as the length of the journey, the dangers travellers might face and the kind of life which would await them in Oregon. The teacher asks if any of those

present have already travelled in the West and some of
the class claim knowledge of the dangers and difficulties
of the journey. The teacher's attitude is positive and she
minimises the dangers they are likely to face. She also
stresses that those who decide to go must be hard-
working and responsible people, because only people
of this kind will survive.

The teacher does not rush the class towards a decision at this point, but asks them to think very carefully
before making up their minds. They must consider
what the journey will mean to them and what they will
be leaving behind. They will meet again to make their
final decision (pp. 37–39).

Now there is a wide open structural trap here for all
the participants, including teacher, for inherent in this
scene is the assumption that it is leading to a decision –
and decision-making, as every chess player and bridge
player knows, is an important element of the game. But
in this particular lesson the decision structure is something of a mirage, for as we have already pointed out at
this stage the situation is not real enough for these children to be making anything but a superficial gesture –
going through the motions of making a decision. Some
may say yes and some may say no and it will have all the
appearance of a decision being made, but the real structure may have been no more than the bland
question/answer relationship between the teacher-in-role
and the class. There is no real momentum to be drawn
from the structure, other than the poor teacher pushing
it along. A momentum will be found only if a *state of
tension* is created for the participants to provide a dynamic
to the action. Such a state of tension can only be achieved
by implanting a hidden structure which must be integral
to the situation – and to what the class can understand
of the situation. The authors give a hint as to what that
structure might be, in their comments:

> The status of the pupils in the activity can be raised
> and the value of their contributions recognised by

suggesting that some of them may already possess considerable information and experience (pp. 36–38).

There is an implied structure here to do with a competitive outdoing of the teacher's role by the pupils in terms of information and experience. But there may be a more useful structure implicit in the teacher's role itself – as government spokesman. Tension can be created either by the sponsor's subtle, superior position of detachment: 'I am only here to *describe* the problems; you are the ones who will have to *face* them', or, quite differently, a hint of 'I know more than I am going to tell', or its cruder version: 'I am doing a good salesman's job and you are going to fall for it'. There are thus four versions here that can be expressed in game structure terms.

(1) Difference of status based on information and experience.
(2) Incompatibility of vested interests.
(3) Relative power.
(4) A trap – to be recognised, avoided and exposed.

Now the teacher entering this role may not be at all clear which of these or mixture of these or other structures is going to be appropriate. She will respond intuitively as she senses the class's needs, or, rather, she may have to respond to the class's *wants*. If the only way to give the drama momentum is to allow through (1) an emergence of crude competition between the teacher and pupils or through the even cruder 'I'm the baddy not to be trusted' approach of (4), then she may have to abandon altogether her intention to open up (2), the recognition by the townsfolk that here is an official who cannot know and indeed who does not want to know what the cost of this decision will be to those of us who are faced with it.

The point that I want to reiterate here, before extending this concept of structure theoretically, is that in the drama process the surface meaning of the event, the meaning which in fact would play a large part if we were to tell it as a story – 'And the townsfolk listened to the Government representative and they had to come to a decision' – may not provide the required game structure. The drama may not be a 'decision-making game' at all. The real structure is a hidden dimension within the material, making connections with their present intellectual and emotional understanding. If it is not found and harnessed, no tension will be felt by the participants and the experience will have no natural momentum. One hears so many discussions *in the name of drama* from children in role as town councillors arguing about building a swimming baths or an old people's home. Unless such a discussion in role is backed by real concern about the outcome, there will be no game. It will be no nearer drama than a debate – although the participants and their teacher may deceive themselves quite happily. On the other hand, if we look at a later decision-making episode in the same project when the pupils are temporarily in role as Indians who have to decide whether or not to receive a white stranger into their midst (p. 53), this is more likely to have been played seriously as a real game for by then the children, after several lessons on the same project, were steeped in the material sufficiently deeply to respect the rich complexity of the problem.

Having given this example of structuring I perhaps need to make clear some of the terminology I have been using before looking at more examples. I am using 'structure' (and specifically *interactional* structure) to mean the mutual relationship between elements of a dramatic event. The term structure is taken from the physical world where objects relate to each other differently. One could say that iron filings relate to a magnet in a different way from cork to water; that a man, bat and ball have a different relationship from man, butterfly net and butterfly. One might also want to note similarities in relationship. Such a relationship can be described as structural, that whatever occurs between the above elements is controlled within the parameters of that structure. Another example would be that two parallel lines have one kind of structure, but two lines that cross have quite a different structure – and whether they are straight or curved in turn affects the structural relationship.

I am suggesting that this relationship is also to be found in games, in the arts and in life. There may be little structural difference, broadly speaking, between a goalkeeper guarding his goal, Cerberus guarding the gates of Hell, and a soldier on duty outside an army barracks. In each case there is a definable relationship between a guard and what he is guarding. Now structure is an abstraction. Some structures can be expressed thematically. For others, as in this example, we seek a language form of definition: we call it a 'guarding' relationship. But when we observe two or more elements and we wish to define a relationship between them, we often turn to a third form of abstraction: *we project a feeling quality onto the relationship*. We eschew mathematical or linguistic (at least of the propositional kind) coding and turn to our feeling response. Thus we say that the feeling quality between two parallel lines is different from the feeling between two lines that cross. We may say that when a piece of music unexpectedly changes to a minor key this expresses a feeling of foreboding. It is not of course the case that the interaction between the major and minor keys actually has this quality – indeed there is no interaction as such – we project that feeling quality onto the structure. (Someone from a different culture may interpret it quite differently). This projection of feeling onto a structure is often given the generic term 'tension'. When in football someone takes aim at the goal we say there is a sudden heightening of tension; when it is all over after a noble save by the goalie there is an equally sudden slackening of tension. When I wrote earlier of the broad structure of 'The Way West' exercise being 'slack', I am really projecting a quality suggesting lack of tension onto the structure.

Another way of putting it is that whereas structure denotes a relationship between the elements of anything, tension denotes our *experience* of structure. As Robert Witkin (1978) explains, tension/structure provides the universal in seemingly dissimilar artefacts. He writes:

> The symmetries and ordering of sensate life in tension structures is the profound business of art everywhere. I suspect that if we were to take a sensate tension structure such as the love-hate paradox that lies at the heart of Shakespeare's Romeo and Juliet theme, we would be able to transpose it into different forms each appropriate to a particular culture, and, provided we had the necessary skill of course, we would be able to do this for all cultures in the world. It was certainly done most effectively for one culture some years ago when Romeo and Juliet were transposed into the idiom of youth group clash in modern New York in West Side Story (p. 95).

As Geoff Readman rightly suggests, tension is the critical pivot which gives impetus to both games and drama. Take tension away and there can be no game, no drama. As I have written earlier, in games the structural relationship which implies tension is often explicitly defined. If we look at a random list of typical game structures we shall find that they reflect some of life's common interactions and are obviously just as important in drama.

hiding/seeking	waiting for a turn
winning/losing	delaying
rewarding/punishing	withholding
risking	deceiving
solving problems	status
competing	surprising
blocking	co-operation
choosing	getting caught
planning strategies	hurdles
manoeuvring in a tricky situation	worrying at a puzzle
avoiding a trap	the horns of a dilemma

Notice how each of these structures implies tension for the participants. If we look at some further examples from Cecily O'Neill's and Alan Lambert's *Drama Structures*, we shall see that many group experiences are dependent on these kinds of simple structures.

In a drama about workhouse conditions in Victorian times with a class of second-year secondary girls (13+), the 'status' structure was employed when the girls, in role as inmates, were interviewed by staff whose attitude at best was indifference (p. 117). Given the tension here was one of humiliation, that can be sufficient in itself to sustain the momentum, especially as this workhouse scene comes at a critical point in the sequence structure – for they have already in an earlier lesson experienced the well-intentioned caring of the 'lady' who housed these girls out of pity but was obliged to hand them over to the authorities. The contrast between being in the lady's charitable care and now in the officious hands of the workhouse staff is an important dynamic. Additionally, the teacher structured the interviewing for 'formality'. Individual 'members of staff' (some of the pupils) were at separate desks with small queues 'waiting their turn'. Thus within one scene we have: status, contrast, formality and waiting one's turn making up the 'game'.

In a subsequent lesson the following episode is described:

The visit

Whole group

The inmates are summoned together by the staff for an important announcement.

The workhouse will be visited by one or more very important people – perhaps a magistrate, an inspector of workhouses, or a wealthy benefactor. The workhouse must be presented in the best possible light. If the inmates do not co-operate, their few existing privileges will be taken away.

When the staff feel that the workhouse is ready for inspection the visitors arrive. The teacher, still in role as Warden, shows them around, and entertains them to tea. Is it possible for the inmates to make the visitors understand what life is like for them, without arousing the hostility of the Warden? Can they bridge the gulf between the visitors and themselves? The visitors may be indifferent to the inmates, or they may be horrified at their plight and wish to help them (p. 119).

The key to the underlying tension here is in the line: 'Is it possible for the inmates to make the visitors understand what life is like for them without arousing the hostility of the Warden?'

Thus embedded in the scene is the 'risking' and 'manoeuvring' game. Can they convey something to the visitors without being seen to do so? I am often asked what skills children have to learn that are specifically drama skills. Since this has cropped up here I would just like to draw attention to it. A class that is good at drama will intuitively recognise that the drama lies in the *difficulty* of conveying that message to the visitors – that is the tension to be enjoyed. Inexperienced pupils will not appreciate either what is essentially dramatic nor the importance of confining any strategies they employ to solve the problem within the logic of the highly status-bound situation. In other words there is always the danger that an inexperienced class, given too free a hand, will fail to give themselves any kind of dramatic or authentic experience. The misguided teacher might well believe that self-expression was all that was needed!

Sometimes in drama a teacher deliberately sets up a structure that appears to lack any obvious game element. I recently watched Dorothy Heathcote, halfway through a lesson on preparing for robbing a bank, release some junior school pupils into a free-play experience where they were to go down a manhole and then search the sewers under the bank. She remained in role at the manhole, available as an ear to their reporting-back if they needed it. Otherwise they were on their own, 'playing', but not playing a *game* for there was no structured game to play. It *appeared* to be a game – of finding things down in the sewer. But you can only play that particular game when in actuality there is something to find. All they found was whatever was in their imaginations (not to be despised of course, but the reality of finding something is not available). Any tension experienced was not in the interactional elements of the scene but in the *psychological* strain of finding an inner logic to their searching. What they allowed themselves to find had to fit logically with the knowledge about sewers they had acquired in the first half of the lesson. A symbolic reminder of the need for this kind of logic was carried in each child's hand – blank paper with which to make notes and sketches of sewer designs.

It is interesting here that we have in Dorothy Heathcote's lesson an example of apparent free-play. The lesson, the drama, the learning all appear to be at risk because of the relative lack of structure. But, of course, Dorothy knows in those particular circumstances it was not a risk – the mental parameters fixed by the first half of the lesson controlled the freedom of the second half – and any individual child who could not cope could turn it into a 'reporting to the boss at the manhole' game. Thus, if he needed that status structure it was there for him.

Now a 'searching for something' or 'exploring' theme crops up a great deal in drama and there are many teachers who do not recognise that what looks like a tense, exciting, well-focused structure may be no such thing. Sometimes you can elect to use this loose form because, as in Dorothy's lesson, the preceding work is strong enough to carry it. At other times you may knowingly take the risk. In the next example Cecily O'Neill and Alan Lambert knew only too well what the dangers are. The sequence is with thirteen-year-olds in a drama about a Lost Valley. Item 8 in the sequence is described as follows:

The pupils join up in small groups to make a tentative

exploration of their environment. Each one may be made responsible for a specific task. For example, seeking out water and food, looking for suitable places to make a shelter, gathering wood, or identifying sources of danger (p. 93).

Typically of experienced teachers recognising the potential weakness of the whole venture (it will in fact only succeed if the pupils are determined to *make* it succeed – not something one can often rely on!), precautions were adopted such as warning them beforehand to mark out the route they take, and (the final card up teacher's sleeve as pupils start to get killed all over the place) to come in as narrator saying, 'Suddenly, for no apparent reason, the danger passed and the members returned to safety'!

The basic problem is that the 'givens' are not clear enough. Every good game defines the parameters of what may or may not be seen as a legitimate action. Exploring the terrain or even setting up camp leave too many things wide open. Compare this with a 'puzzle' structure used by the same authors with a similar age group of children who had asked for a 'horror mystery' drama.

The Mystery

Whole Group

The teacher explains that he will be asking the class to work as one group. He will take on a role as the head of a special unit in a hospital, and they will need to adopt the roles of experts whose help is needed in dealing with a particular patient whose case is causing him great concern. It presents a mystery which he cannot solve.

The pupils seat themselves in a square representing the doctor's office. He greets them in role and apologises for breaking into their busy professional schedules. He hopes that the discussion will not take up too much of their time, but assures them that their advice and guidance will be of great importance. He reminds them of the confidential nature of the case: nobody is to discuss it outside the room. He then gives them the following details.

Narrative Link

'There is a young child in my care at this hospital, who is seven years old. She was brought here several days ago following a mysterious incident at her home. One morning her parents found her sitting outside her bedroom door. When they entered the room they found it to be in a state of confusion. It was wrecked, they said. They asked their daughter what had happened but she refused to speak. She has not spoken since. She is obviously very shocked, though she is physically well. The only way in which she has made any reference to what happened during the night has been in the form of two pictures. She drew them yesterday. The first one shows her bedroom in its usual state. The second one shows it in the condition in which her parents found it when they went in there on that morning a few days ago' (p. 156–7).

The 'head of the special unit' then proceeds to show the pictures as evidence for the children to discuss and draw hypotheses from. Now essentially this also relies on the children's using their imaginations to find answers – as in the case of the 'sewer' and the 'Lost Valley' contexts – but the difference is that (a) each 'find' is given due weight and attention, is publicly shared, evaluated, accepted or rejected, (b) the focus within which their imaginations can have free range is defined from the beginning, i.e. the puzzle is clear – 'what could be a logical solution?' is the name of the game, and (c) the problem-solving does not have to be hurried by action.

Of course, the success of this lesson has to do with more than structure (indeed, I am not suggesting that structure is all a teacher needs to know about!). In passing, let us note the 'elegance' of this particular focus chosen by the teacher. The class wants something to do with 'horror mystery'. The teacher does not make the mistake of finding a game that has all the stereotype trappings of horror and mystery. He finds a symbol – two simple drawings – which are intriguing enough to activate each pupil into endowing them with whatever his or her own personal interpretation of horror might be.

Sometimes a most carefully planned game structure is ineffective because it is not for some reason appropriate either to the material or to the particular class. Included in a report of a National Association of Teachers of Drama conference (1981) there is a detailed account and analysis of a lesson with a group of young adolescents on the subject of a holy community living in twelfth-century Durham Cathedral. The game structure the teacher planned was a neat 'horns of a dilemma' situation where the community's wish to keep their cathedral as a place of sanctuary was to be challenged by the presence of a refuge-seeker who, they suddenly realised, might be the perpetrator of a vicious crime against their own kind. But all games are dependent on the players having some degree of understanding of the concepts involved. This particular game can only work if the concept of a vow to give sanctuary is something the participants already have a vested interest in. Implicit in the notion of a game is that of taking a risk, and one bases one's decision on what it will cost if one loses. If the children in Durham Cathedral do not have a sense of what it would cost *them* to break the vow of sanctuary they cannot have much interest vested in keeping it. Thus what looks like a perfect example of a 'horns of a dilemma' structure, turns out not to be so – it was a game that could have been played two or three lessons or ten lessons later. In other words they needed to experience the 'sanctuary game' before they could cope with a 'breaking of sanctuary game'.

Sometimes it is valuable *literally* to include a game within the drama experience, and I will finish this subsection with such an example.

Alan Lambert, in setting the atmosphere for drama about Beowulf, proceeds as follows:

Moving round the circle, the teacher faces each pupil

in turn and takes their hand in a special handshake. He asks each one to say the oath with him. When he has returned to his place they all repeat the oath in unison. He holds up a stick for all to see. This, Beowulf's stick, will be their standard.

He reaffirms his pleasure at once again seeing so many of his loyal friends. He has called them here to listen to his news. He tells them of a tale he has heard, of how a monster called Grendel has killed many of Earl Hrothgar's people. Some of those present say they too have heard this story and speak of what they know.

Beowulf says that he would like to sail for Hrothgar's land and take up the fight against the monster. He knows that many of those now present will be eager to go with him on this adventure, but first of all he would like to present them with a challenge. Will they be prepared to undertake some tests which he has devised? He needs to be reminded again of his companions' great skills. The tests are designed to illustrate those qualities which may be essential if the adventure is to be a success (p. 207).

And then the teacher unequivocally plays a game – a game within a game, if you like:

> Grendel is a cunning monster. It may be necessary to set a trap for him. Stealth will prove to be a valuable asset; it has often been so in the past.
>
> In role teacher places a chair in the centre of the circle. Under it he lays down a stick ('Beowulf's stick'). The test is quite simple. Whoever volunteers will be asked to remove the stick and take it back to his or her place without making a noise. Another member of the group will be sitting on the chair with eyes closed and will point in the direction of the slightest sound. The attempt fails if the volunteer is caught in the process of removing the stick.

The teacher adapts a fairly well-known game to serve his purposes here, generally known as 'Keeper of the

Keys'. (In its traditional form, a bunch of keys is placed under the chair in the centre of a large circle. The 'keeper' sits on the chair and is blindfolded. A volunteer tries to retrieve the keys without being caught out and, if successful, becomes the new 'keeper'). Since the teacher has already used a stick as a sign of Beowulf's authority he decides to give this additional prominence by making it the object to be retrieved from under the chair. The person from whom it has to be taken becomes the 'guardian' of the stick. The teacher occasionally provides a commentary which anticipates the kind of adventures in which the followers may become involved: 'Our standard has fallen into enemy hands but the one who guards it is now asleep. It will take an act of stealth and courage to rescue it. See how well our companions perform this undertaking' (p. 207).

The dramatic playing mode of the 'game' of drama

We are now in a position to examine the kind of behaviour that is appropriate to the 'game' of drama discussed in this chapter. Not unexpectedly it is the kind of role behaviour to be found in the ordinary playing of games. A participant in a game adopts a role based on his conception of others' roles, what George Herbert Mead (1934) calls the 'generalised other': a child cannot play hide-and-seek unless in 'hiding' he understands the function of the 'seeker'. His role only exists in terms of the other roles in the game. As Lawrence Stenhouse (1981) puts it, there has to be a *mutuality*. This is true of role in a game and role in the 'game' of drama. John Smith only functions as a goalkeeper when there are others who continue to endow him with that function. The Durham Cathedral players will only function as protectors of the cathedral and of refugees seeking asylum in so far as others in the drama expect that function from them. The child who is cast in role as abbot of the cathedral is not identifying with some fictitious character called 'Abbot', he is merely taking on an abbot's function *vis-à-vis* the situation of being in charge of other people in the community, just as the football captain in a game is not playing a 'character' of a football captain, he is functioning in the required role of being in charge of his team.

This view of acting behaviour as no more than role function has taken us a long time to understand. Most drama books write of children 'playing a part', 'playing someone else', 'taking on a character', whereas what is required of children in drama (or at least, in the dramatic playing mode) is that they be themselves, functioning in whatever way the situation demands of them. It might require them to behave authoritatively, submissively, wickedly or shrewdly; the role might be labelled explorer, prime minister, designer or archaeologist, but they will do no more than adapt functionally to the situation of the drama just as they would adapt to roles required in a game – just as they once learnt to adapt to the limited number of roles imposed on them in real life. In drama, of course, the range and subtleties of roles are far greater than in games or in life. Because of this the skill required is often very challenging, *but it is not the skill of the performer; it is the skill of bringing oneself to function with a degree of maturity that one's normal 'life' role does not demand.* Sadly, this is what Arts educationalists like Malcolm Ross (1978) would deny our children, for he can only perceive of drama as a Performing Art.

In fact the mode of behaviour required has little to do with performing other than keeping open the normal communication channels between people as players do in a game. A goalkeeper does not 'perform' his function in its theatrical sense, only in the sociological usage of 'perform' which we shall be looking at further in the next chapter. The same applies to the child 'performing' the abbot's function. This is, of course, what is meant by dramatic playing as it was defined in Chapter Three, the mode of dramatic behaviour espoused by Peter Slade. The participant makes a choice to enter make-believe play, a game or drama (all three require an 'as if' gloss, although in the game form it is rarely explicit – charades might be the exception); he enters the make-believe play, game or drama with the intention of temporarily 'bracketing off' practical life so that he might experience this specially contrived 'present'. It is happening in the present, and the future can only be guessed at. It does not have the fore-knowledge of the story form. A goal may or may not be scored; the abbot may or may not admit the refugee from justice.

I am emphasising the existential quality of dramatic playing here because it is in direct contrast to the expectations of acting behaviour to be found in some educational institutions. For instance, America is the only country that has seriously attempted to measure children's drama. If the CEMREL Research Project (1972) is any indication of what is expected it seems American teachers are looking for a child's skill at 'showing', and, in particular, 'showing' emotion. A recent book on evaluation in education (Hamilton et al., 1977) quotes from the project:

> The teacher gave simple instructions to 'listen, watch arms, body, etc.'. The first three children were sad, happy and surprised in turn. The sad girl rubbed her eyes, commenting 'Oh, I'm so sad'; the happy boy exuberantly jumped up and down and commented 'Oh, I'm so happy. The sun is out'. Later, anger and fright entered the parade (p. 318).

Later we read a quotation from what is called a 'characterisation package':

> Some of the boys as well as the girls were quite stiff and unable to use their bodies to convey and represent the emotions being expressed in the material from the composites [i.e. Characterisation package]. Again, the point I want to make here is that the perceptual, cognitive understanding of the expression of emotions in non-verbal ways from pictures, cards, etc. is very different from the expressions of the materials with one's own hands or face or body (p. 320).

The article goes on to quote from Michael Polanyi who, I am sure, would have been horrified to see how intent these researchers are on isolating emotion as something to be 'switched on' and 'portrayed'. This kind of drama for practice in expressing and communicating emotions is far removed from the functioning behaviour required in the game of drama, where the participants' concentration is not on whether he or she is signalling an emotion but with getting on with solving whatever problem is to hand. 'Characterisation packages' are in my view a total irrelevance to drama and to education. I think there are many American teachers who would agree with me, but those kinds of 'packs' have an unfortunate way of creeping onto the desks of teachers who do not know any better and the resulting work may not only be irrelevant but harmful.

But there are those in England, too, who also fail to see that participation in drama has two faces, or rather, a face and a mask: the 'game' of drama where a group of participants *share* a significant experience, and a theatrical performance where a group of actors *present* the drama so that an audience might have a significant experience. 'Face' and 'mask' may still be the wrong metaphor, for it is too rigid, denying the fluid state of continual re-moulding, and it also denies those rare but important occasions when mask and face are indistinguishable. On the other hand, if we confine our view of drama to that of performance art we may so love the mask we overlook the face. Likewise it would be equally regrettable if in finding so much satisfaction from the face, we withheld from our children the artistry of creating a mask.

Summary

In this chapter I have attempted to show that early experiences in England of Religious Drama were partially equated with a 'game' or a 'pastime' and as such avoided the charge of blasphemy or sacrilege. Its apparent non-seriousness became its safeguard. Authorities could condone the 'playing the game of the Passion'.

I suggested that there is a whole range of 'play' activities or second-order experiences which are 'bracketed off' from the practicalities of day-to-day living, activities such as games, art, rituals and celebrations which are man's way of creating order. Normal criteria of serious/non-serious, true/false are not relevant.

The common ground between games and group drama can be expressed either anthropologically (they are both a form of group celebration) or structurally. I identified three kinds of structures: sequential, interactional and psychological. It is the interactional that I examined in the chapter in some detail.

The view of creative drama in schools as a 'game' of drama has implications for how we should perceive acting behaviour. In both games and drama a participant *chooses* to play. His intention is to experience an 'as if' context – in a game two friends may agree to behave *as if* they are opponents; in drama two friends may make exactly the same agreement. The participant adopts whatever role *function* is required of him by the context.

A performance mode is inappropriate in the 'game' of drama, for a performance mode is concerned with *representation*. I used an inadequate metaphor of 'face' and 'mask', suggesting that performing is more akin to creating a mask for someone else to look at. Such a metaphor denies the dynamic character of performance which, for instance, can be changed by an audience's response.

We shall look more closely at the relationship between the dramatic playing and performance modes in the next chapter.

6 Emotion and the game of drama

I have just been watching on television the final scenes from the Royal Shakespeare Company's performance of *Nicholas Nickleby*. Poor institutionalised Smike is taken by Nicholas and his sister to their childhood home in Devon. As they look at what was the garden where they played as children, Nicholas reminisces, 'We used to play hide-and-seek here, Smike' The incredulous Smike asks, '*You* ... Hide!?' 'Only the game,' assures Nicholas. 'Play' is beyond Smike's comprehension. He knew only too well the pain of really hiding from someone.

In a game the pain of life can safely be recaptured, encountered and switched off as required, for as we have seen, a game and all other forms of playing including the arts are deliberately created second-order experiences, removed from the rawness of living. The substance of the playing is an abstraction. In hide-and-seek, a number of people agree for a period of time to abstract from living what they know of the 'hiding' function (i.e. that people can be 'hiders' and 'seekers' and that places can be 'hiding places') and to behave, for the time being, as if only that function mattered. In drama a number of people agree to abstract from what they know of the 'hiding' function and to combine that knowledge with what they have understood about a particular 'hiding' context, say, King Charles and his followers hiding from the Round-heads (hiders are therefore labelled Cavaliers, and the seekers Roundheads) and to behave 'as if' only that func-tion mattered. (The prime difference between the two is that in the drama there is no need *actually* to hide – the hiding experience is evoked but not practised. The secondary difference between the two is that the dramatic context of King Charles opens up an elaboration of reference points which the simple game does not require.)

The emotional quality of the game experience has been characterised by Vygotsky as having a dual affect. He says, '. . . the child weeps in play as a patient, but revels as a player' (p. 549). But this is, I believe, slightly misleading, for although he is right about the mixture of often contradictory emotions, it is wrong to give the impression that the weeping is of the same order of emotional experience related to the child being a patient in actuality. I wept when Smike died in the television play, and I recall an incident of a nine-year-old girl turning to a particular page of *Black Beauty*, crying bitterly and explaining through her tears to her grandmother, 'It's so s-a-d!' But neither of these was close to the grief we would have experienced in the real presence of death. The emotional response in a game, play and in drama is a *response to an abstraction*, to a 'bracketing-off' from living, and it can be just as intense – possibly even more intense for, knowing it is a second-order experience, one can 'release' one's grieving, for example, in a way one would not do in the actual event. If Smike were to play in a drama that required him to hide from someone, the pain of suddenly being found might hurt, but not with the rawness nor with the permanence of actuality. And of course, the hurt as Vygotsky suggests would immediately be tempered by the pleasure of knowing 'it's only a game'.

But the pain is nevertheless real. This is the basis of all imaginative acts, that through emotion something absent is brought into the present. Margaret Sutherland (1971) puts it succinctly:

> Emotions occur in response to actual happenings; they occur also in response to imagined happenings; and the latter emotions are real, happening in the present, even though they are called up by unreal situations. In fact, we give a kind of reality to imagined creations by feeling these emotions; in a way we live an imagined situation because it affects us emotionally. (p. 5)

When I read a novel the emotions aroused in me bring the experience of the events of the narrative into the present, but I am not likely to be misled into thinking it is actually happening for there are enough indicators in the environment to assure me that it is not. On the other hand if I am in a drama experience my own actions and things about me may trap me into believing I am in an actual event. The infamous Stanford Prison study experiment (Haney et al., 1973), which had to be stopped because students in role as either prison warders or prisoners forgot they were in role, is powerful evidence of this possibility. Drama and make-believe play, unlike other second-order experiences, can look like a real event because of the concreteness of the medium. A headmaster friend told me recently that he had burst into a classroom mistakenly thinking some pupils were up to no good, only to discover it was drama; and I recall one of my own students, in playing the role of a prisoner-of-war camp commandant berating the 'prisoners' and warning them that he had ways of finding out where the missing prisoner was if he didn't own up, was somewhat taken aback to hear the voice of the school caretaker call from the other end of the drama hall, 'There's a boy here, Mr. Ainscough, skulking by this radiator'!

Geoff Gillham (1979), in a paper read to a Cockpit Theatre Conference in 1978, raises the question of why young children are not generally confused by the two. The answer he gives is that the child freely enters the make-believe world secure in the signals from the real world that the real world is continuing to exist. Thus we have the paradox that in order to give oneself over to believing in the fiction, one's 'non-belief' has to be secured. Geoff Gillham expands on this point:

> What is it that allows such belief to occur in the child when so much, to the observer, is unreal? Examine a scene from the play where one boy creeps up on another and then springs on him stabbing him in the back with his knife. The knife – the crucial prop here

– is visually represented by a fist clenched as though round the knife handle. The sign is adequate for the make-believe (the metaphorical reality) to occur. I can enjoy the experience of killing or being wounded fully, because I am *not* killing or being killed. If the sign were a wooden stick, care would have to be exercised in not hurting or being hurt – the mechanism of the make-believe being blurred by the intrusion of the present objective reality. If the sign were a real knife, clearly the knife would no longer be a sign but the thing itself ... The make-believe is short-circuited and made impossible ...

The creation of a metaphorical reality is achieved through the process of extracting from the present objective situation signals and signs appropriate to an absent significant reality, for use in the construction of that absent reality within the present situation.

BUT

Belief in the metaphorical reality can only be achieved if *other* signals in the present objective situation affirm that the metaphorical reality is *not*, objectively, the absent reality for which it stands (p. 3).

Gillham continues to argue that just as the participant is protected from physical hurt by the parameters of 'it's only a game', so the same protection applies to psychological hurt. In view of our discussion above I would like to qualify this and to suggest that there can be a degree of psychological hurt, however fleeting, inherent in the experience. When a young child plays 'What time is it, Mr. Wolf?', she may experience a moment of panic when the 'Wolf' shouts, 'Dinner time!' and chases her. When the 'Wolf' catches her he may obey the laws of the game and avoid physically hurting her, but giving her a momentary fright is a legitimate part of the game. Indeed it is fairly common for very young children to invite Daddy to be the Big Bad Wolf in order to test the boundaries between reality and make-believe. The very ambiguity

108

between real and not real can have its own frightening fascination.

One of the important differences between a game and drama is that in the latter the signals between reality and fiction may be less clear. A classic example is when the teacher within the fiction assumes an authoritarian role which follows too closely to what the children see as teacher's normal role pattern. At such times a child is required to have a very strong grip on the nature of the 'game' if she is not to be deceived – or the teacher wisely keeps coming out of role in order to establish the difference for the child. A teacher working with a class she does not know needs to signal reality rather more strongly than when class and teacher are used to each other. Where the edges between reality and fiction become blurred, there is a danger that the emotion felt is first order, that is, unmediated by abstraction or knowledge of pretence.

The balance between a game and reality is a delicate one, as Huizinga points out:

> ... as soon as the rules are transgressed the whole play-world collapses. The game is over. The umpire's whistle breaks the spell and sets 'real' life going again.
>
> The player who trespasses against the rules or ignores them is a 'spoil-sport'. The 'spoil-sport' is not the same as the false player, the cheat; for the latter pretends to be playing the game and, on the face of it, still acknowledges the magic circle. It is curious to note how much more lenient society is to the cheat than to the spoil-sport. This is because the 'spoil-sport' shatters the play-world itself. By withdrawing from the game he reveals the relativity and fragility of the play-world in which he had temporarily shut himself with others. He robs play of its illusion – a pregnant word which literally means 'in-play' (from *inlusio, illudere,* or *inludere*). Therefore he must be cast out, for he threatens the existence of the play community (p. 30).

If a conventional game can appear so fragile, how much

more so does drama with its less explicit rules. We have shown how drama may suffer if there are insufficient signals to remind the participants of the real world but there are other factors which may deter entry into the dramatic fiction. Prominent among these is lack of spontaneity for which there may be a number of reasons, two of which may be characterised as (1) a high degree of vested interest, and (2) a high concern for one's reputation. Let us first look at spontaneity generally.

Spontaneity

Both J. L. Moreno (1964) and Peter Slade rightly emphasise the importance of spontaneity. It suggests being sufficiently 'within' a situation to allow one's intuition to work. Lack of spontaneity suggests a high degree of calculation, looking at a situation as if one was not really part of it. As we shall see in the next chapter, arriving at a balance between these two is often what drama educationalists are seeking.

Another way of describing lack of spontaneity is to say that the participant is 'holding back', not 'letting himself go', not 'giving himself' to the situation. One of the prerequisites of second-order experiencing is an element of initial *submission*: it requires a passive/active engagement. For instance, I cannot actively engage with a book unless I am mentally free to give myself to it – if my mind is on other practical affairs while I am reading or if my reading competence is inadequate then I shall not be able to submit to the experience.

Drama, too, requires an initial act of submission. So important was this factor to Ed Berman that he used to get the participants formally to 'make a contract' to take part before the work started. Most of us who avoid this kind of extreme nevertheless require from our classes an unspoken contract. In Dorothy Heathcote's early days of doing drama with adults she would sometimes begin in role with 'Did you get the message . . .?' And her soleful eyes and wobbling chin would be challenging the others, *daring* them not to join in!

Many kinds of reasons prevail in the drama lesson for participants 'holding back'. They may not, for instance, be prepared to risk having any kind of emotional engagement (I recently worked with a group of headteachers for whom this seemed to be a problem); or they may not trust each other or the teacher; or the 'hidden curriculum' of the group's own dynamics may cut across the drama's requirements (for instance if the strong natural leader within the group is not given her usual leadership function within the fiction); or the group may concentrate too hard on preparing material for 'showing' so that they miss out almost entirely on 'playing the drama game'; or they may dislike drama or really want to perform a play or are simply not in the mood to submit to the experience. Two deterrents to entering drama are of particular interest.

1 High degree of vested interest

One man's second-order is another man's first-order experience. Playing football, telling a joke or making model aeroplanes are normally seen as second-order experiences, unless one happens to be a professional footballer, a comedian or a model aeroplane manufacturer. Sometimes an activity may be both simultaneously. For instance, I can see that writing this book is a function of my job and as such is part of the responsibility of earning a living, but it is also an escape for me, a kind of haven to which I can take refuge from the hundred and one pressures that impinge on the practical business of living.

Now in drama an excessive degree of vested interest in either the technical aspects or in the substance of the subject-matter can upset the balance so that the 'game' of drama and the necessary spontaneity that goes with it disappear. For instance, concern over a drama examination could for some candidates obliterate the possibility of second-order experiencing. An executive involved in a role-play exercise in order to improve his management skills might be so determined to learn that his very effort

111

to do so precludes the necessary 'submission' to the experience. A protagonist asked to play out a scene from her own life in a psycho-drama session may be too anxious about what will emerge to 'play the game' spontaneously. A recent bereavement may make it impossible for a participant in a drama class to join in a drama about the Plague of London or the death of Cordelia. And it is not unknown for members of a group to manipulate a drama to further their real-life victimisation of the class 'scapegoat' – so that it is not a drama experience at all but a vicious first-order experience disguised as drama. For a teacher, of course, drama must be a first-order experience – her vested interest is in the educational and aesthetic welfare of her class.

2 High degree of concern for one's own image

Rom Harré, a philosopher and social psychologist, argues there are but two dimensions along which a man acts: the practical dimension which directs his maintenance of life (this coincides with my use of first-order experience) and an 'expressive' dimension, which he sees as the 'over-riding pre-occupation of human life' (p. 3). This second dimension is concerned with the individual's need for honour and reputation. He states: 'The most persistent theme of this work will be the thought that for most people at most times the expressive order dominates or shapes the practical order.' In conducting his social analysis Harré seems to give little if any attention to play, games and the arts. It may well be he would argue that all these things are but part of the private man's attempt to gain public approval. And there is a sense in which this applies, but although I can appreciate his point that seeking a good reputation may well dominate the practical order, if it were also to dominate the activities I have designated 'second-order' then it makes nonsense of the possibility of 'disinterestedness', enjoying something for its own sake. However, I am happy to concede that seeking public approval might well at times override and thus eliminate 'disinterestedness'. If my attempt at writing this book was solely or even largely done with public approval in mind, then my 'haven' image becomes an illusion. It is not difficult to think of other examples – the man who takes up golf to be seen with the 'right sort of people' the competitor more interested in the prize than the process of winning it; the senior common-room member who cannot converse without showing off. But the balance is a delicate one, for even the golfer, the competitor and the staff member may become 'caught up' and absorbed in the thing itself and enhancement of reputation may at least temporarily be held in abeyance.

The implications of this peculiar kind of vested interest, interest in one's public image, for drama are probably obvious – the participant who wants to be seen as a good actor, for example. For others it may be the opposite problem, that doing drama is 'a bit silly', a childish game, and that to take part is to 'lose face'. Sometimes the substance of drama seems to lower one's prestige in the eyes of others – for instance, being in role as a 'loser'. It often happens that young children find it enormously difficult to 'surrender power'. I can recall a class of eight- to nine-year-olds in Brisbane in which one or two could not cope with being in a submissive role of being hi-jacked. One boy had to 'solve' the problem straight away by suddenly producing his own gun, even though intellectually he recognised that the 'rule of the game' was that the passengers were unarmed. Likewise it is sometimes difficult for adolescent boys who work hard at building an image of toughness within their peer group to drop that image for the sake of the drama. Indeed, a teacher must respect the need adolescents have to be protected from being made vulnerable by the drama. Later we shall be looking at ways in which a teacher might deal with this problem. We shall see, for instance, that it is the modes of 'exercise' and 'performance' that are more likely to give this protection than 'dramatic playing', unless, as we shall see, the dramatic playing is *projected*.

Before we can assess fully the relative merits of dramatic playing, exercise and performance modes, it will be necessary to re-define the relationship between them, particularly from the point of view of emotion.

The relationship between dramatic playing and performance

So far I have been at pains to make a clear distinction between these two modes. In Chapter Two I asserted that two contrary intentions are involved: the intention to *be*, to submit to the experience of an event, and the intention to *describe*, to communicate an event to someone else. In terms of emotion one could use a grammatical analogy (see Bolton, 1978) that the 'occurring' emotion expressed by a participant is a *verb*, whereas the emotion portrayed by a performer is descriptive, an adjective, no less. Such an analogy helps to reinforce the distinctive orientations of the two modes. Theoretically, it is conceivable that, say, experiencing regret (the verb) at having made a wrong decision and depicting regret (the adjective) are a different genre. The verb is spontaneous, fluid and not repeatable; the adjective is calculated, static and repeatable. The verb is subjective, hidden; the adjective is objective, explicit, worn like a badge on one's sleeve, a 'sign' of regret. Empirically it is valid. Two such distinct behaviours can at times be observed, either by the participant himself or by an outside observer. As a participant I can feel the difference between genuinely regretting something and signalling such a feeling. To achieve the latter I have to see myself as an object, to know how my regretting might appear. An outsider, too, can often distinguish between a child 'lost' in what he is doing and a child intent on 'showing' what he is doing. We have an example of the latter in its crudest form in the Cemrel Project already referred to on page 102, where each child is required to display a variety of emotions as part of a test. Not only does the boy 'wear' the appropriate external features, he uses words to enhance his simulations: 'I am so happy' is his way of making sure the observers get the message!

But having made the distinction clear between the two modes it is necessary now to acknowledge that to see the relationship always in terms of contrary orientations may be an oversimplification. Although I am anxious to avoid entering into aesthetic theory or acting theory to any large extent it has to be conceded that the topic I have been tackling here, the logical relationship between emotion occurring and emotion described has been of central interest to aestheticians and acting theorists alike. For instance, Susanne Langer, in most of her writing on Aesthetics has been concerned to establish that emotion expressed through Art is derived from but is not the same as that felt in real life. Typically, in her third publication (1975) on the subject she writes:

> . . . what the creative form expresses is the nature of feelings conceived, imaginatively realised, and rendered by a labor of formulation and abstractive vision (p. 90).

Any emotion an artist feels undergoes a sea-change. If he is sad, then his art expresses a sadness, as Ivy Campbell-Fisher (1950) puts it, 'released from the entanglement of contingency' (p. 267).

But I would like to note in passing that Mrs. Campbell-Fisher's observation could be applied to *all* second-order experiences, not just the arts. For example, sadness felt within a *ritual* could also be an emotion 'released from the entanglement of contingency'. What Susanne Langer is saying, however, does seem attributable solely to the arts. Very few aestheticians, however, look at acting as a phenomenon – Edward Bullough (1912), in his work on Psychical Distancing, is perhaps the notable exception. (May I also draw the attention of the reader to my own writing on this subject [Bolton, 1977].) The major theorists on acting, on the other hand, such as Diderot (1957), Stanislavsky (1937), Brecht (1973), Craig (1962), Artaud (1970) and Brook (1968) tend to be interested in a particular theatrical style while writers on theatre such as Weissman (1965) and Barish (1966) choose to write about acting from a psychoanalytical point of view.

I wish to rely on a model, both elegant and simple, expounded by a philosopher, Alan Tormey (1971), which seems to be not entirely incompatible with most aesthetic and performance theories. I am grateful to Ken Robinson (1981) for drawing my attention to Tormey's writings on Expression. His thesis is that there is a double valence to behaviour − expressive behaviour which implies a state of emotional arousal and representational behaviour which 'detaches the surface of emotional behaviour', not itself involving arousal. (This, of course, is compatible with the above verb/adjective analogy which Tormey incidentally also employs.)

Expressive behaviour, according to Tormey (and not to be confused with the way Harré is using the term) points in two directions simultaneously: towards some state of emotional arousal in the person (say, anger or wonder or pleasure); and towards what he calls an intentional object, something outside the person to which the state of arousal is prepositionally related. (I am angry *over* an act of injustice or I wonder *at* the sight of Niagara Falls or I am pleased *with* my Christmas present.) We might well be inclined to call this intentional object the *context* of the emotional arousal for it is the cognitive relationship with a particular context that gives the emotion its particular characteristics. There is really no such experience of an emotion called anger − there is only *my* anger, in *this* context, on *this* particular occasion. Notice also that expressive behaviour in this definition does not distinguish between voluntary and involuntary behaviour. If I jump with surprise when a dog suddenly barks at me, my behaviour is no less expressive than if I shout at it to shut up. Both entail a subjective-objective relationship.

The critical point is that in expressive behaviours of all kinds, verbal, non-verbal, voluntary, involuntary, there is an aspect of the behaviour that remains hidden, only known or felt by the person experiencing the behaviour.

In representational behaviour, on the other hand, all the meanings are made explicit. For Tormey one of the 'purest' instances of representational behaviour is that of an actor who rages on stage as Lear but who could not possibly be expressing his own rage or he would never complete the performance. Denis Diderot writes:

> If the actor were full, really full, of feeling, how could he play the same part twice running with the same spirit and success? Full of fire at the first performance, he would be worn out and as cold as marble at the third. (p. 14)

According to Tormey, the actor is in fact depicting the *character's* distress, not his own. In other words, the actor's behaviour is *not* expressive. What the audience is watching is Lear's expressive behaviour, not the actor's. Tormey extends this point to all art. A painting, a symphony or a play is not expressive of the artist or the performer – it is expressive of itself. This is not its weakness but its strength: all meanings are made explicit (or rather 'embodied' would be a better term, for 'explicit' suggests the exactness of a diagram, a map, a formula or a tele-gram) within the art product. There does not remain within the artist hidden meanings only known to himself. His skill lies in *representing* his deepest feelings, not expressing them.

When Tormey cites the art of acting as an example of representational behaviour, he was really talking about the style of acting first attributed to the famous English eighteenth-century actor David Garrick, acting which demanded not the expression of emotion but an accom-plished technique by which 'natural' expressions of real life became distilled on stage by artifice. For Diderot, an admirer of Garrick, the key to acting lay in its repeata-bility. It is the actor's art to find the conventional sign. As Richard Sennett (1974) puts it, 'A feeling can be conveyed more than once when a person, having ceased to "suffer it", and now at a distance studying it, comes to define its essential form' (p. 112).

It would make the writing of this chapter easier if I could call a halt on this discussion of the relationship between dramatic playing and performance and change the topic. I could then conveniently sum up by pointing out that these various non-educational theorists in introducing concepts such as representation, distillation and repeatability reinforce the importance of the distinction I have drawn throughout the book, for clearly dramatic playing is expressive (in Tormey's usage), spontaneous and not amenable to repetition. Regrettably it is not as simple as that. As we probe further it will become more and more necessary to re-assess the relationship between the two modes as dialectical rather than that of opposites.

This is partly brought about by the theoretical writings of Constantin Stanislavsky who confounds the issue for us by bringing emotional expression back onto the stage. Indeed Charles Marowitz (1978), a director working in the Stanislavskian tradition, refers to acting as 'An Act of Being', a phrase too reminiscent of dramatic playing for us to ignore it. Before tackling this particular challenge to our thesis, let us get off our chest two other similarities.

1 Both dramatic playing and performance use dramatic metaphors, abstractions which immediately qualify the kind, intensity and degree of emotional response – one can reasonably assume that neither the actor on stage nor the child in the classroom is actually going to experience murderous intent, overwhelming grief, spiritual ecstasy or sexual arousal during the drama experience. Thus even if an actor, following Stanislavsky, allows himself to become emotionally engaged during a performance his emotional response, mediated by dramatic form, can only be an approximation to the character's supposed emotional state.

2 Another aspect which the two modes do appear to have in common is that in neither mode is the participant required to concentrate on the emotion itself (another reason why Cemrel has got it wrong). Just as the child in dramatic playing concentrates on the task or the problem to be solved, so the advice from Stanislavsky to

his actors is that concentration should be on the mainspring of *action* in the character's behaviour, not his feelings. (A misinterpretation of Stanislavsky on this very point, it is interesting to note, gave Lee Strasbourg's 'Method School' its distinctive training.) But Stanislavskian actors are nevertheless concerned in rehearsal and other preparation time with tapping their own reservoirs of emotional memories to find within themselves a sophistication, subtlety or depth of emotional engagement so that in concentrating on the character's actions, a wider, deeper range of emotions may be released.

It is this concern of an actor to build a character and to extend his own emotional repertoire which puts the above attempt to draw a comparison between dramatic playing and performance into a proper perspective. What a long way we have suddenly moved from the point argued in Chapter Five, that in dramatic playing the participant is adopting a *function*. As I then pointed out, finding the character of the Abbot is what the child in the Durham Cathedral play is not required to do. If we are to admit similarities between the two modes we must not forget differences such as this that remain fundamental. Nevertheless, we shall find there is common ground, but we need first to pursue the Stanislavskian actor a bit further.

For Charles Marowitz the actor is by definition 'someone who remembers'. I propose to quote his definition in full:

An actor is someone who remembers.

On the simplest level, someone who remembers his lines, his cues, his moves, his notes, to do up his fly-buttons, to tie his shoe-laces, to carry his props, to enter, to exit. Simple things, complex things. An actor is someone who remembers.

On another level, an actor is someone who remembers what it felt like to be spurned, to be proud, to be angry, to be tender – all the manifestations of emotion he experienced as a child, as an adolescent, in early manhood and maturity. An actor remembers the 'feel'

119

of all the feelings he ever felt or ever sensed in others. He remembers what happened to other people through all periods of recorded time – through what he has read and been taught. In tracing the lineaments of his own sensibility, he has the key to understanding everyone else.

On a deeper level, an actor is someone who remembers the primitive primordial impulses that inhabited his body before he was 'civilized' and 'educated'. He remembers what it feels like to experience intense hunger and profound thirst, irrational loathing and sublime contentment. He recalls the earliest sensations of light and heat, the invasion of infernal forces and the coming of celestial light. He remembers the anguish of disapproval and the comforting security of guardians.

He remembers vividly (not necessarily articulately) what it feels like to be isolated, to be partnered, to be set adrift, to be reclaimed. He remembers that miasmic stretch of time before becoming aware of the details of his own identity. He remembers the world before it became *his* world and himself before he became his self.

To be without memory and to be an actor is inconceivable. An actor is someone who remembers (pp. 26/27).

I have quoted this passage in full, not because I think it is particularly inspired or even well-written, but because it is the nearest attempt I have come across to suggest some of the subjective, hidden meanings that might well make up a performer's luggage when he expresses himself on stage. For there can be no doubt that Expressive behaviour as understood by Tormey – a state of emotional arousal in a person relating prepositionally to an object (or person) outside that person – is seen by the Stanislavskian School as a proper way for an actor to behave on stage. He may scorn, tease, insult or placate his stage wife and have appropriate feelings as he does so (bearing in mind the necessary modification we have already admitted, but modified or not, the response is an emotional one).

We have then two schools of thought in connection with emotion and performance. In their extreme forms the 'techniques' school would have it that an actor's performance is detached from his own feelings during performance, that he represents a distillation of what he understands of the character's feelings; the Stanislavkian actor, on the other hand, becomes emotionally involved as he performs his role. It is the latter view which at first sight seems to challenge Tormey's theory, for any 'expression' by the actor implies a subjective/objective relationship, the inner meanings of which remain hidden from the audience. But this is to misunderstand Stanislavsky, for the sophistication of the 'Art of the Actor' lies in the skill of making those very subjective meanings available to an audience. The actor may while he is on stage feel deeply, say, some of the emotional references listed by Marowitz, but Stanislavsky demands that they be simultaneously translated *through technique* into a form that touches an audience at its deepest level of feeling. In other words, ultimately even Stanislavsky is concerned with *representation*, in keeping with Tormey's view of all art. The two schools of thought then do not diverge to the extent that has first appeared. As Michael Goldman (1975) suggests, fashions in acting can be seen in terms of the varying degrees to which it is thought proper to expose the private feeling of the actor. That such a choice between working emotionally or technically can be made is useful for teachers to be aware of. For instance, Dorothy Heathcote, in working on the Minamata tragedy towards performance, required the sixth form 'actors' to remain emotionally detached from their roles, an example of 'protection' from personal exposure to which we shall be returning later.

It seems we can now qualify our position on the relationship between dramatic playing and performance modes by saying that although the ultimate intention of the performer is to 'describe' an emotional event, the quality essential to dramatic playing, the quality of 'being' may also enter the performance mode, given the Stanislavsky approach. In such cases the first signs of a dialectic occur: the actor is both experiencing and describing; an oscillation is set up between these two incompatible grammatical constructs, the verb and the adjective. The actor, in attempting to subject himself spontaneously to an occurrence and at the same time communicate that occurrence to an audience, is experiencing an unresolvable tension. It seems, however, that the tension for the actor is but derivative of that tension endlessly defined and redefined by psychiatrists, psychologists and social psychologists in terms of inner/outer reality: I/Me, Ego/Self, or subjective/objective. It can be argued that the art of the actor is but a sophisticated reflection of what occurs in all human action: a struggle between what is privately felt and symbolically controlled (using 'symbolic' in the sense of the 'public language' of number, words, gesture and sound, etc.), a perpetual state of disequilibrium between personalising and objectifying.

It might be thought that the actor's art also reflects the continual struggle between participants in a *social* situation to share their private worlds through public media of language and gesture, what Arthur Brittan (1973) refers to as 'negotiation of meaning'. This, however, is only partially the case. Quite obviously the playwright has largely pre-empted negotiation of this kind; also, a theatrical performance can hardly be said to be a social interaction in a normal sense as the actor's concern is to describe to someone *outside* the interaction on stage – to the spectator. Dorothy Heathcote (1982), writing in SCYPT, that fine journal for Theatre-in-Education companies, begins the opening paragraph with:

> Actual living and theatre, which is a depiction of living conditions, both use the same network of signs as their medium of communication; namely the human being signalling across space, in immediate time, to and

with others, each reading and signalling simultaneously within the action of each passing moment. We cannot help signing so long as there is another human being who needs to read the signs. Actions become *sign* whenever there is more than one person present to read the action (p. 18).

She is right to draw our attention to the importance of signalling in both 'actual living and theatre', but it should not be assumed that the same kinds of signs are employed in these two contexts. The actor is operating virtually in a one-way communication pattern with little room for negotiating. His signs have to be of a special kind, directed at non-participants in the fiction.

But if we turn now to look at dramatic playing we see that that particular mode does indeed reflect the private/public tension in *all* respects. The individual is caught up in the personalising/objectifying dialectic as in life, and because the communication is between participants, the normal interaction of a social context is also reflected. Participants are free to 'negotiate meaning'. In both living and in dramatic playing a participant is continually accommodating to an image of himself as an object in order to communicate with others. This is the essence of participating in a social environment. To do this he has to employ language and gesture appropriate to the context in which he finds himself – he may shout 'Halt!' or give a salute on an army parade ground, but not at a picnic. In other words there is a publically accepted code of conduct which he is expected to *perform*. When the army sergeant salutes his officer he is performing, giving the conventional sign that describes the hierarchical relationship between the two men. Likewise as I pointed out in the last chapter, in dramatic playing a boy may be required to adopt the function of an Abbot of Durham Cathedral, and in so far as he continues to see himself in that role he will continue to signal to others that that is what he is doing. In other words he will be *performing* that function, and his words and gestures will be selected with the intention of describing to others what he is doing. Dramatic playing, therefore, like life, contains elements of the performance mode. But we have been using the term 'performing' for what the actor does – an act of describing to non-participants who are present as spectators. In life and in dramatic playing the 'others' are fellow participants with whom one is negotiating meaning. The intention therefore is significantly different although both are concerned with presenting oneself as an object of others' attention and finding a public language to do so. Let us retain this distinction from 'acting' by using the term 'presentation' in a sense akin to what Goffman (1969) means by 'presentation of self in everyday life'. We are applying it not to everyday life, but to that aspect of the performance mode that is, at least incipiently, present in dramatic playing.

Let me try to summarise the point we have arrived at in describing this now complex relationship. There are two contrary orientations, pulling in the direction of either 'being' or 'describing'. Neither of these is pure; their relationship is dialectical, each having within itself an element of the other.

A. *Dramatic playing*, therefore, is continually in a state of tension between personal expression and finding the public means of presenting oneself, using language and gesture, in order to communicate to the others taking part. The more heightened the form of that communication, as we shall see in the illustration that follows, the nearer the participant is to reaching the performance mode *within* dramatic playing. The most extreme form of dramatic playing would be egocentric play.

B. *The performing mode*, therefore, is continually in a state of tension between representing (describing) an experience and actually submitting to 'being' in the experience. The most extreme form of representation will appear to be entirely technically achieved, and the actor's own emotions will be irrelevant. The most complex form of representation is where expression (dramatic playing) in the actor exists alongside his attempt to represent to an audience the character's expression. This Stanislavskian approach requires both considerable sensitivity of feeling and technique.

The element of performance referred to under *Dramatic playing* occurs as part of a participant's expression but it has such clarity and selectivity of communication to other participants that it acquires the 'adjectival', descriptive characteristic of performing. To distinguish this from the actor's concern to communicate to non-participants, we have used the term 'presentation'.

If we use a diagram to summarise the relationship it needs to be shown as a polarity, a pull in opposite directions with an imaginary half-way mark balancing the two.

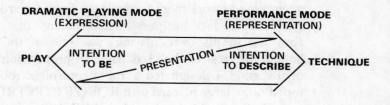

The implications of this dialectic for the teacher are considerable. Such a conception allows for a greater fluidity between the two modes than has hitherto been found acceptable. In the past, as we have seen in earlier chapters, teachers have either confined themselves almost entirely to one or the other of the modes (using terms like 'creative drama' in opposition to 'theatre') or they have seen them as separate stages in the child's education. I am suggesting that within the one *is* the other – in some respects a Chinese Box would have provided a better diagram than a polarisation continuum, although it would have been difficult to decide which box should be on the outside. This does not mean that I am now suggesting all children should have the chance of performing a scripted play in front of an audience (indeed I doubt whether many young people are likely to be mature enough to cope with the sophisticated Stanislavsky approach to performance). What I am suggesting is a more subtle movement between the two.

I need to give an example. My most recent teaching before I started on this book was in Vancouver with a class of mixed ages – ten to thirteen years, I guess. An instance of the kind of fluidity I have in mind occurred for one boy who was in role as a 'robot controller'. Each time he went into action it was a very private experience for him. He followed his robots (two children as robot nurses) around, whispering instructions to them and occasionally taking over and doing the tasks for them as he found it difficult to be precise in his instructions. This was an example of dramatic playing, made more pronounced to those of us watching by the fact that the rest of the class were attempting to work more formally – edging towards 'presentation'. In fact his persistent signalling that he was absorbed in his own 'playing' was one of the factors holding the rest of the class back. In preparation for the final session, I designated a 'robot controller' room area, roped off, a large placard with ROBOT CONTROLLER in red (I should have added PRIVATE, DO NOT ENTER as a nice re-inforcer of the point, but I did not think about it in time) against a dais on which stood a table and a hand microphone (a television control device which he had carried around with him on previous occasions). Thus the pressure on him to find what Dorothy Heathcote usefully calls his 'public voice' was considerable. His robot companions were now to operate well away from him across a fairly large room and at key moments in the drama when there was an anticipatory silence from everyone else, he found he had the personal 'power', and with some verbal style (and a high degree of repressed excitement as he discovered he could be publicly effective) he *presented* himself as an efficient robot controller. *He had broken through from dramatic playing to a kind of performance*, a 'presentation', a subtle combination of personal expression and public code. As a teacher it was very important that I recognised this was the new experience he needed. If I had confined myself to initiating 'creative drama' or 'improvisation', I might well have remained satisfied with his participation for he was indeed meeting all the requirements of dramatic playing.

In giving this example, I do not wish to imply that the relationship between dramatic playing and performing is developmental – far from it. There will be times when the movement will be in reverse. For instance, a group of adolescents intending to look at how a family might drive one of its members to suicide, began their drama by working out the family's relative positions round the graveside, concerning themselves with 'how it would look if it were a still photograph'. From the stillness achieved each was then formally (theatrically?) to speak a line of dialogue which would betray an attitude to the dead young woman. After this performance the class was ready to move to the much more difficult task of using the naturalistic interaction of dramatic playing to explore how the family related to each other in day-to-day living.

Notice this latter illustration concentrating on the externals of a still picture and then having selectively to use a 'public voice', carried less risk of inadequate work than if the group had gone straight into dramatic playing, a mode which is often used indiscriminately and without any kind of rigour. Preparing the way for dramatic playing by first setting up performance and/or exercise modes is often a very necessary part of teacher's structuring. Indeed, as we shall see in the final chapter, one of the principal skills a drama teacher requires is the ability to recognise the potential and suitability of each mode for the particular topic and the particular group and to recognise that the incipient performance mode in dramatic playing and the incipient dramatic playing mode in performance provide the means for an imperceptible movement between the two. Perhaps the key factor which leads the teacher to make a decision on where to start and how to continue is that of 'protection', a concept to which we need to devote the final section of this chapter on emotion.

Protection

I cannot stress enough how important it is for teachers to realise that because drama is such a powerful tool for helping people change, as teachers we need to be very sensitive to the emotional demands we make on our students. The notion of 'protection' is not necessarily concerned with protecting participants *from* emotion, for unless there is some kind of emotional engagement nothing can be learned, but rather to protect them *into* emotion. This requires a careful grading of structures toward an effective equilibrium so that self-esteem, personal dignity, personal defences and group security are never over-challenged. I shall discuss three kinds of protection: (a) performance mode, (b) indirect handling of the topic and (c) projection.

1 Performance mode

Performance mode has its own kind of built-in protection. One way of using it, as we have already discovered, is to treat the pain of a funeral gathering as a technical exercise. In other words, instead of trying to simulate grief or whatever, the emotional aspects are held in abeyance in order to make decisions about the external features of the depiction. There are many advantages of working this way, two of which are that the performance technique required is minimal, well within the abilities of the class to achieve a satisfactory result from their point of view, and that it allows the class and its individual members to control the emotional input. If they wish they can stick to the bare bones of the task, as an intellectual exercise, but if they feel secure they may inject 'feeling' ideas.

The second structure, involved in the line of dialogue round the graveside, is more exposing, for it really tests each participant's commitment to the affective aspect of the event. But each is still strongly protected by the very *form* of the performance mode. It is stylised, abstract. It would have been far more threatening to have attempted a simulation of a 'round the graveside' dramatic playing.

Briefly, then, for we shall be returning to this same point later in the book, it can be said that the performance mode itself can be protective, either because it is seen to be mainly a technical or intellectual task, or because the dramatic form is powerful enough to enhance whatever the participants' contribution might be. Sometimes the strong sense of form causes individuals to rise to the occasion or if they do not, their inadequacy can be contained by the form itself.

2 Indirect handling of topic

Some subjects are painful, sensational, controversial or just a bit too exciting. This is not a reason to avoid them for drama more than any other activity in school can help children find a mature approach to such topics. But to handle them *directly*, that is, to open up the central issue that arouses the pain, sensationalism or the controversy is not necessarily the best way of protecting children into emotion. Indeed, with some topics if the teacher does not handle them indirectly, the class will hastily protect themselves by opting out, fooling around, etc.

There are three ways of dealing with a topic indirectly. One is to enter a drama at an oblique angle to the main issue. For instance, I recall David Davis being asked by his class of adolescents if they could do some drama about prostitution. After discussing what led a girl to become a prostitute they then set up a series of dramas showing some of the stresses (including poverty) a fictitious character had had to face in her early life.

Likewise in setting up a drama for an already excitable ten-year-old class on their chosen topic of a haunted house, I spent the whole of the first lesson as a pub proprieter refusing to show them how to find the house. Of course, such a device is doing more than protecting them from an over-exciting adventure; it is also in a calmer way building up their anticipation of a real mystery. For these young children the haunted house gained in significance as they tackled the immediate problem of the bloody-minded landlord – just as in the 'prostitution' lessons a more respectful attitude to the problems of prostitution grew as the adolescents actually centred their attention on 'where poverty can hurt'.

Another, more popular, way of working indirectly is to place the participants in a role that only obliquely connects with the topic. Dorothy Heathcote is very fond of employing this structure. 'Mantle of the expert' for example, is almost by definition a way of working from an angle of detachment. (Protection is not its only value, of course – others will be discussed in the final chapter). Thus in our 'suicide' drama the adolescents, instead of being in role as members of the family concerned, could have been neighbours or reporters getting a good story. In the 'prostitution' lesson, instead of being in role as the 'other poor people' sharing the girl's life, they could have been social workers, town councillors or students on a counselling training course. The 'haunted house' drama could have had its 'investigators from the British Poltergeist Society'.

A third way of dealing with a topic indirectly, perhaps the most difficult to handle, is to use *analogy*. It is difficult, for any misjudgement in the planning by the teacher can seriously affect the validity of the parallel that is being drawn. The simplest form of analogy is to change the historical setting for the event, for instance, attempting to place The Good Samaritan in a contemporary setting, or doing the reverse of this – taking some contemporary problem such as racism and setting it in past times, in a context between, say, the Jews and the Samaritans or the Greeks and the Romans. On the other hand, the apparent dissimilarity can be stretched even further (say, using the Odysseus and the Sirens story for the topic of drug abuse) providing the teacher takes care to ensure the group makes the right connections!

3 Projection in the dramatic playing mode

Central to Peter Slade's theory of child drama was the distinction he made between personal and projected play (or drama). He writes:

> Throughout the whole of life, Man is happy or unhappy in so far as he discovers the right admixture for his life of these quite distinct manners of using energy. Both the type of person and the life occupation are connected with the balance of Self and projection (p. 35).

It is his recognition that projected activities draw upon a distinctly different kind of energy (and I include emotional response) from non-projected activity that I think is of fundamental importance. His classification into personal and projected play represents a hierarchy of abstraction; dramatic activities using oneself as the medium of expression standing at a lower level on the table of abstraction than dramatic activities using media other than oneself. I would like to extend his thesis in order to establish that the dramatic playing mode can use both personal and projected activity. To avoid confusion of terms, I prefer to refer to the activities as either projected or 'non-projected'. A hierarchy table could look like this:

Let us take the activity of running.

It is the projected activities, the group under E and F, which will concern us in this section, as we shall see that it is projection which protects the participants. I have divided E and F according to whether they are actively engaged in projecting, i.e. either making something or merely percipients of a 'running' stimulus, a much more passive role. Quite obviously the passivity of, say, looking at someone else's drawing is considerably less demanding than doing one's own. Both are projected activities, for in each case one's attention is directed *away from oneself*, which is of course what offers the protection.

	A. The activity of running	concrete (no abstraction)
NON-PROJECTED	B. Running to hide as part of a game	first level of abstraction
	C. Running 'as if' in a drama	second level of abstraction
NON-PROJECTED	D. Running in a mime performance	second level of abstraction
PROJECTED (ACTIVE)	E. Drawing a runner Sculpting a runner Making a sound tape of running feet Writing a story about a runner Directing a mime performance of running, etc. etc.	higher levels of abstraction
PROJECTED (PASSIVE)	F. Looking at a photograph of a runner Handling a sculpture of a runner Reading about a runner Watching a play or a film about a runner, etc. etc.	higher levels of abstraction

(a) Passive projection

Examples might include having case-study documents of the new intake available as a starting point for a drama about prison; a huge map for a drama about Treasure Island; and architect's designs of Paris sewers for a drama about a bank robbery (I referred to this lesson in Chapter 5). The list can go on and on: contents of a hand-bag; pages of a diary; newspaper cuttings; an epitaph; school record cards; photographs of housing demolition; map of a street; artefacts of any evocative kind.

An important extension of this 'passive' list is Dorothy Heathcote's use of a second 'person-in-role' (in addition to the teacher) – a tramp, a soldier, a stowaway, Christopher Columbus, etc. One of the advantages of using a person-in-role over inanimate objects is that the 'passive' stage of watching and listening can gradually change to a more active involvement, as and when the class seems ready, but more important of course is the extra dynamic edge that is brought to the whole occasion by having present someone real and breathing and tangible instead of just a photograph. One can use both of course. Chris Lawrence, in working with a class of London children, showed them some photographs of 'dancers' whom the children were later to meet and instruct on the movement of animals. The class spent considerable time examining these photographs, attempting to anticipate the kind of personalities they were to be working with. Such is found to be the effectiveness of having a second person-in-role (usually another teacher) that Newcastle upon Tyne Drama Advisory Team have cultivated the idea of offering a 'character' to the local schools (they call it 'Rent-a-role', so that a class in a primary school, say, working on the topic of The Peasants' Revolt can – with sufficient notice of course! – ask one of the team to come into the school as Wat Tyler). One of the most fully documented projects of this kind is Dorothy Heathcote's (1980) work with a nine-year-old class on Dr. Lister (see also *The Treatment of Dr. Lister* by John Carroll (1980)).

It will be seen that the variations on this passive kind of projection are infinite. It does not, of course, have to be the first stage of the drama work. Injecting a different perspective of this kind part way through a project can also have its uses. The important point is that it should be used at a time when for some reason pressure is to be taken off members of the class – putting them in what is virtually a 'spectator' role can give them time to recover from what had perhaps been inadequate non-projected work. I say *virtually* a spectator role, for the teacher is likely still to endow the pupils with a role label – 'I have a patient outside. I have asked you senior staff here for a special reason. I would like you to watch me interview him' – immediately lets the class off the hook of having to participate in the normal way. Notice they are not only given a *reason* for observing, which, of course, gives their spectator role a frame through which to watch, but there is also a hint of some responsibility they might have to carry – a necessary engagement is then ensured.

(b) *Active projection in dramatic playing*

It would be less passive, but still a form of projection, if in the above illustration I were to add, 'And doctors . . . if you wouldn't mind making notes . . . to help our discussion later'. In doing this I have further controlled the quality of attention to be expected *but* it still protects the participants because the centre of their attention is away from themselves. Likewise, if instead of saying, 'there is a patient outside', I could say (out of role), 'In a short while I will be a patient coming to the consultant's office – how do you want me to play the role? For instance, when I am sitting on this chair, how do you want me to appear? etc., etc.' (I recently watched a more formal version of this technique where a class of adolescents was invited to direct the teacher in how to appear as a King of a small Greek State in classical times who had lost his power to a conquering neighbouring state but who did not want to lose his dignity. The group would be more than spectators for now they have to make active decisions. Their attention is still projected – in this case through the 'modelling' they are doing on the teacher.) There is, of course, an enormous difference between the private/public demands of the two examples: writing my own private notes protects me rather more than having publicly to make suggestions on how the teacher as 'patient' should, say, knock on a door. The teacher who knows her class will judge best which of these projections the class will be most comfortable with *or* will be most challenged by. For the other side of the 'protection' coin to be wary of is *over*-protection.

In the illustrations of projection so far I have suggested that broadly speaking there are two kinds: (1) where the participants are allowed to be passive observers becoming more actively engaged as and when they wish, and (2) where from the beginning the participants are required to *do* something. Both of these strategies can keep non-projected dramatic playing at bay for a long time if necessary. I can recall a class of ten-year-olds designing their own Norman village for several drama sessions before they became engaged in non-projected drama activity (personal play, as Peter Slade calls it), i.e. before they started interacting with each other *as villagers* instead of *through their designs*. Notice both activities qualify as dramatic playing for both carry the intention to 'be', to be either designers or villagers, both working spontaneously and appropriately within their quite different functions.

It is not always easy to switch from projected to non-projected drama. The projected can feel so secure – there is often so much less personal risk in being in role as a 'headmaster' examining and discussing case-study documents of a school truant than being involved in 'reprimanding a school truant'. One of the ways of making a bridge between the two is to use teacher-in-role.

(c) Teacher-in-role

The most subtle strategy available to a teacher is that of teacher-in-role, for this device is flexible enough to have any one of the three functions; it can take the pupils' attention *off* themselves by allowing them passively or actively to use teacher's role as a projection, or it can be non-projective and challenge the pupils to interact. It is relatively easy to move from one to the other. I can give an illustration of what I mean. When I asked a class of five-year-olds what they would like to 'turn me into' for a story, they said a witch, and added, a very wicked witch. Thus they had a chance *actively* to project onto me whatever 'wickedness' they had in their minds. I did not carry out their instructions very well so they had to be very precise in explaining things to me. Some of their instructions included reading a spell-book in my witch's house, which had, we established, a door close to where the children were sitting.

135

I moved to a different phase and involved myself in witch-like pursuits, looking for a special spell (they had already told me what it was to be). Thus, for a few moments they reverted to *passive* projection, in role merely as spectators of teacher's performance. Now my responsibility is to bring them a *non*-projected activity. The remarkable thing about teacher-in-role is that it allows the teacher to change into a different gear, as it were, as subtly or as crudely as the occasion seems to require. In this particular instance, I casually 'looked through my window' and muttered to myself that I thought I saw 'some people' outside my house. This single action and comment implied a huge transformation in but one simple step, for suddenly we were on the edge of non-projected activity – 'some people outside my house' places the children in a markedly different relationship to the drama. They are in danger of losing their spectator status. The tension rises as they sense the difference. I moved to the door and 'opened it' an inch. They felt very threatened, although 'opening the door of my house' had been one of the actions tried out when the class was directing me in how to be a witch. But the meaning has changed, for now *they* are included in 'dramatic time' and are much less protected. Notice how the first step of looking through the window is less threatening than the second one of opening the door. The window distances to some extent; the door exposes the alarming feeling of not only sharing the same dramatic time but the same dramatic space. So I 'open it *an inch*' and thus I delay further, giving them time to take it all in and to adjust to the exposure to what they must ultimately cope with: the witch addressing them directly. This careful bridging from projection to non-projection is yet another skill a teacher needs to acquire.

Thus the teacher-in-role can decide from moment to moment whether to carry the burden of the pupils' protection – 'My men (a group of 'passive' children) have *this* to say to you' is to be totally protective – or to remove that protection and hand over the power: 'My men have something to say to you . . .!' Let us conclude this section on protection by tabulating our analysis.

Protective techniques
Performance: Technical
Formal
Indirect: Oblique approach to topic
Distanced role
Analogy
Projection: Passive
Active
Teacher-in-role

Let us look at a sequence in a recent series of lessons with the Vancouver children already referred to earlier in this chapter. In the first session the group chose the topic of hospitals in the future. Three phases in the first lesson were as follows:

(1) Designing, in small groups, some special machines to be found in hospitals in the future.

Because they were not enacting any kind of simulation of hospital life, the exercise could be described as INDIRECT.

It was also indirect in respect of role distance – they were 'designers', not part of hospital life. Because their concentration was actively on something other than themselves it could be described as ACTIVELY PROJECTED.

(2) The class was asked to instruct me and one of the pupils in how to behave as a reporter and doctor respectively, the reporter wanting information from the busy doctor about 'these new machines' he had heard about.

This has moved into the DIRECT – a doctor who is using one of the machines is involved. But it remains as ACTIVELY PROJECTED – a totally different kind of projection, of course.

(3) Half the class became 'doctors' and half remained as

'designers'. A public discussion was held between the groups, the designers explaining how the machines would work.

This is an extension of the scene they had directed at 2, but they were now all in it. The finished designs, although offering partial projection were not sufficient to take away the focus of attention from the participants themselves, for they were now all in 'dramatic time'. This was therefore DIRECT AND NON-PROJECTED.

These are three simple and fairly obvious examples of protective devices with a topic that did not of itself require careful handling, but when at the end of the lesson they chose to extend their interest in hospitals in the future to 'finding a cure for cancer' quite suddenly the subject-matter has become more of a delicate one, with some taboos attached for both the pupils and the adults watching the lesson. Thus in my planning for subsequent lessons, the person in the drama who might die of cancer *was never played by anyone in the group*. A chair was placed in a certain spot in the room for each lesson – Theresa's chair. Theresa was a six-year-old girl who was going to need our scientific skill and our love. We saw her doll, always with her on the arm of the chair, but Theresa was never there. She *became there* as the week went on and as we seriously, intently were able to talk to her and even comb her hair.

We built up a *projection* of Theresa, and Theresa's cancer became very real. This is what I mean by *protection* – we did not run away from the terrible topic: the use of projection allowed us to *face* cancer.

Summary

In this chapter we have argued that emotion in drama is real, but that it is nevertheless a modified version of that same emotion felt in an actual event, for the emotional response in drama is a response to an abstraction. It is also accompanied by the dual affect of satisfaction in creating the drama. The emotion felt, although heavily qualified, can be equally or even more intense, as for all second-order experiencing.

For a child to feel free to respond to a make-believe situation, there must be sufficient signals in the environment reminding him that the real world continues to exist. 'Submitting' to the experience is a necessary step which a participant may be deterred from taking for a number of reasons, particularly if he has too great a vested interest in the subject-matter or in his own reputation.

According to Tormey's theory of Expression, emotional involvement for the actor is minimal. Such a theory would seem to support the notion of two distinct orientations of dramatic playing and performing, but Stanislavsky's theory of acting seems to embrace both modes, leading us to consider the model as *dialectic*, each mode containing the seed of its opposite. In looking, therefore, for a possible performance element within the dramatic playing mode we discovered that a certain heightened form of dramatic playing, which we labelled *presentation*, occurred when a significant contribution by a participant was communicated by words and gestures achieving a shared public meaning. At such moments participants find their 'public' voice and do not need the kind of protection they may have relied on earlier.

We discussed the concept of 'protection' as protection *into* emotion not from emotion. We looked in some detail at some aspects of protection which included certain kinds of technical and formal *performance*, the *indirect* handling of painful subjects and *projection*, the latter including some aspects of the teacher's most flexible strategy, *teacher-in-role*.

7 Drama as experience – aesthetic and educational

I have been at some pains in other recent publications (Bolton, 1979, 1980 and 1982) to draw attention to what I perceive as common ground between drama for learning and drama as an art form. Perhaps the controversy round this subject is best illustrated by two articles by Malcolm Ross and myself (his is a postscript to mine) in *The Development of Aesthetic Experience* (1982) and in my follow-up paper read by me at the Barbican Theatre in November 1982 (1983). In putting my case for an eclectic view, I have tended to focus on how the teacher in the classroom is handling the same 'clay' as the playwright or the theatre director. What works effectively for an audience at a basic theatrical level will equally well operate for the spontaneous drama of the classroom. I have made the mistake in the past of saying that both teacher and director are therefore using theatre. This usage of the term 'theatre' has been confusing. It would have been more sensible to say, as Ken Robinson (1980) does, that teachers, pupils, directors and actors are using the same medium of *drama*. This allows the term 'theatre' to continue to refer to the *occasion* of presenting something to an audience. However, although I still hold the view that the same clay is being used by the two different sets of people for different purposes, I wish in this publication to attempt to map out a psychological rationale for drawing connections between drama as an aesthetic and as an educational experience.

Let us begin by looking closely at an example of a 'participant-in-role', taking the very ordinary situation of an interview where the interviewee waits for her turn to go in to be interviewed. Pedestrian as this appears to be, there is nevertheless within the occurrence of the role-play some of that very quality that stirred the priests and congregation in '*Quem Quaeritis*'. As I said in Chapter Five, 'Whither goest thou?' uniquely transforms the *narrative* of the Bible story into the dramatic *present* and the dramatic *presence*. Granted, 'waiting for an interview' does not have the spiritual awe of the church celebration! But it does have its own special vitality. The move from talking about an interview, picturing, reading about or thinking about an interview to 'enacting' (to use a term from John Norman (1981)) an interviewee is akin to 'quickening' in the mediaeval sense. Bringing to the here and now an event which is not really in the here and now has a very deep fascination for us. Even this modest attempt at make-believe is invested with the power to arrest attention. Teachers and trainers who use it will know what I mean when I suggest that observers of such 'ordinary' role-play (especially if it is occurring physically close at hand) often watch with a considerable degree of attention. It is all to do with the 'magic' of the dramatic present and presence. This guides us to the essential nature of the dramatic medium: it is a special act of imagination on the part of the participants and of either a formal or informal audience. Participants and percipients engage with what is going on by holding two worlds in mind at the same time, what Augusto Boal (1981) calls 'metaxis', an interplay between the actual and the fictitious. The role-player is actually sitting there on a chair; the interviewee is not 'real', but we respond to her 'as if' she is.

A central thesis of this publication is that the dual consciousness of metaxis (or 'as if') is a form of mental liberation. R. K. Elliott (1973) speaks of all imaginative acts as a means of freeing ourselves from our circumscribed view of the world. He writes:

> Imagination breaks the domination of our ordinary habits of conception and perception – including aesthetic perception – which seems to bind us absolutely to the given world (p. 113).

Of all the kinds of imaginative behaviours, however, drama is the only one that articulates inventing, anticipating, recollecting, hypothesising, creating, musing and day-dreaming or any other mode of imagining through the medium of concrete action. Thus breaking 'ordinary habits of conception and perception' is achieved in a unique way, through the particularity of an occurring event. In this lies the dramatic medium's potency as an educational tool. Teaching is a process concerned with breaking, challenging, supplementing or eroding a child's present achievement in conception and perception and 'as if' behaviour can be the teacher's most effective tool for doing this.

Dramatic activity does not supersede direct experience nor is it a second-best to direct experience. Its potency lies in 'metaxis', a heightened state of consciousness that holds two worlds in the mind at the same time. The fictitious world is not 'given', to be merely suffered. It is actively *construed*, so that submitting to its experience is tempered by the treatment of it as an *object*. Thus the psychology of dramatic behaviour is of a different order from direct experience and independent of any criteria to do with 'nearly real'; it is a form of experiencing that 'brackets off' an occurrence, permitting both submission and an enhanced degree of *detachment*. This view is far removed from Peter Slade's emphasis on Absorption – 'being completely wrapped up in what is being done or what one is doing, to the exclusion of all other thoughts' – which tends to underline the 'submission' aspect of dramatic playing, as does the phrase 'living through' used in the early writings of Dorothy Heathcote. As Dorothy recognised the essential double valence of experiencing and reflecting on the experiencing of dramatic action the less she clung to the notion of 'living through'. Indeed in the way she now persists in working for detachment, she has been likened to Bertolt Brecht in the theatre (Fiala, 1980).

Dramatic action as a tool for learning then rests in its capacity (1) to separate and objectify an event and (2) to break down established concepts and perceptions. The implications of this view of drama and learning will be returned to later in the chapter, for here we need to continue to look at the relationship between drama as an educational and as an aesthetic experience. We will now look back at R. K. Elliott's assertion about imagination (p. 141).

With the insertion by Elliott of 'including aesthetic perception' he is obviously implying two kinds of perception. From this one could conclude that what is being eroded is either the capacity to perceive the given world as an object or in some other way which may be termed aesthetic. Now what is meant by aesthetic? For Arnaud Reid, as we have seen, it is a matter of 'disinterestedness', where an object is attended to 'for its own sake'. I earlier quarrelled with this definition on the grounds that all second-order experiencing, including games and rituals, could lay claim to a quality of disinterestedness. The concept is useful, however, when we wish to distinguish between drama that can be enjoyed as drama, for its own sake, and drama for which there is some under-lying purpose such as learning about interviews. It could be argued that the latter hardly qualifies for being of 'interest in itself'. I am reminded of Robert Witkin's (1974) back-handed comments on this kind of dramatic usage:

> ... and a great many role-play situations improvised in drama sessions in schools have nothing whatever to do with drama although there is no doubt they are a good basis for practical sociology (p. 92).

While recognising that drama as an art or drama as education might usefully be distinguished on this non-functional/functional basis, I want to point out that even in the most mundane use of role-play – sitting in a chair waiting for an interview, to continue with the same example – there is at least incipiently present an aesthetic dimension, for it does use the dramatic present and presence, and it does isolate or bracket off a piece of living so that what occurs within the brackets has to some extent, however limited, become significant in itself. Dismissing it as 'practical sociology' may be to miss the dramatic *potential* of the activity. To understand what that potential might be we need to look more closely at the meaning of aesthetic.

It is noticeable that in describing what is meant by aesthetic Reid does not identify anything about the art object itself, but rather *the way in which it is attended to*. One could read *War and Peace* as an aesthetic experience or as a guide to social life in Russia during the Napoleonic Wars. This tallies with Elliott's use of alternative forms of perception – and Robert Witkin's dismissal of simulated role-play. But do they have to be alternatives? Could not one attend to *War and Peace* both aesthetically *and* functionally? Indeed may not the experience be richer for giving the work both kinds of attention? This is something which of necessity we shall be returning to, but the point I wish to register here is that aesthetic meaning or significance is not an element of the thing created – it is a special quality of attention in the creator or observer. This is not to say that there is nothing special about an object of art, but that what the artist offers are *indicators* open to aesthetic interpretation. The aesthetic meaning is not itself an element. What we perceive are sign-posts to aesthetic meaning. In watching Tom Stoppard's play, *The Real Thing*, we notice that the play begins with an actor building a tower of cards. If we fail to see this simple action as the playwright's 'indicator' to something else our interpretation will remain quite literal and without an aesthetic dimension.

But concluding that the aesthetic is a way of looking at something, does not deprive us of attempting to say what kind of thing we see when we are so disposed to look. If we are to see beyond 'the tower of cards', what do we see? What does the observer or participant in drama gain insight into if he is operating aesthetically rather than functionally? For an explanation of the difference between these two kinds of attention I turn again to Robert Witkin

144

who, in drawing on Rudolph Arnheim (1970), writes as follows:

> When we speak of 'motherhood' as a generalising abstraction, the category of 'motherhood' subsumes each and every instance of what we might term mothering behaviour, etc. When the artist succeeds in depicting 'motherhood' in a painting, however, he does not subsume anything at all. He crystallises a unitary sensate form through which 'motherhood' in all its *particularity* can be known. The generalising abstraction is a 'container' for reality whereas the individualising abstraction represents the very 'essence' of the individual's sensate experience (p. 177).

Although drama uses concrete action and objects as its medium of expression, it is nevertheless an abstraction, as indeed is all second-order experiencing: a particular situation is bracketed off from everyday living. That abstraction can be interpreted in two ways, as a generalising abstraction and as a crystallisation. In the former, the dramatic event is seen as an instance of a more general category. For example, a role-play about an interview is expected to *typify* interview situations. In the latter the meaning of the dramatic event lies in its particularity. *This* interviewee, sitting waiting on *this* chair, crystallises the *essential meanings* of an interview situation. This is the nature of aesthetic intention: to expose the inner meanings of an event, to indicate universal implications. The interviewee on the chair outside a shut door, far from being but an instance of a general case, may now symbolise the isolation, the lack of status, the impotence of being a pawn in the hands of others, the indignity of being stared at as others pass by, the feeling of ordinary life being suspended as one just waits on a chair, etc. The aesthetic intention of drama then is concerned with essences; the functional intentions are concerned with generalisations. Both are expressed through a sequence of events in time – the plot, as it were. The plot itself, however, is neither aesthetic nor functional. Where sole interest is given to the plot either by the participants or by an audience, the degree to which the aesthetic dimension is resonated or the functional dimension of referential meanings is called into being is minimal.

And yet, no greater emphasis has been given to any other aspect of drama in schools than story-line. We have offered our pupils a diet that has been neither aesthetically satisfying nor epistemologically useful. Not many of our pupils in acting out a story could share the sentiments quoted in Chapter Two: 'In the Ancient Mariner we plumbed the depths of experience which are not within the supposed range of children of 12 and 13.' The story form in drama is but a springboard to aesthetic meanings. Many teachers have thought that the enactment of a narrative is an end in itself. We need to find ways of helping our pupils to be open to the aesthetic dimension in their own work and in the realised form of watching a play. However great a work of dramatic art, unless an audience attends to it aesthetically its significance will be missed: *Hamlet* will be seen as no more than a plot about whether a usurping King who murdered his brother will get found out. Sometimes, however, a play can be so powerfully presented that it works on an audience's latent sense of the aesthetic, although actors who have had an overdose of school matinées may feel sceptical on this point. And yet it is something much more than an exciting plot that reduces a noisy cinema audience of popcorn-eating children to total silence at the showing of a film like *E.T.* The aesthetic dimension can be awakened in all of us. However, some would go so far as to say that our present school system of education sets out not to promote but to eradicate it.

There may be a danger that I am sounding pompous about plot. After all, when I am watching a 'Who dunnit?' on television, I am not interested in significant meanings or in learning about detective procedures. I am simply enjoying the plot. But there is another more important reason why we should respect plot for it is the 'what-happens-next?' of story-line that often, as far as the pupils are concerned, gives the drama its dynamic. This point will be returned to in the next section on learning.

Before proceeding, let me summarise the main argument of this chapter so far. I have suggested that the immediate power of drama is that it elicits a basic response in both the doer and the watcher to the 'magic' of bringing something into the present and presence that is not really happening. This suggests that all forms of enactment, even the most ordinary role-play, bear, incipiently, the aesthetic dimension of an art product. The aesthetic meaning, however, is dependent on the kind of attention the participant or the percipient gives to the enactment, and here it is possible to distinguish two contrasted kinds of intention: the intention to perceive the role-enactment in either a functional (a generalising abstraction) or an aesthetic light (an individualising abstraction or crystallisation). If the former, the interest lies principally in treating the enactment referentially; if the latter, attention is given to more essential or universal meanings. It perhaps should be noted at this point that this 'attention' implies an affective rather than a cognitive identification – aesthetic meanings are *felt* rather than comprehended. The universal meanings (or 'import' as Susanne Langer (1953) prefers) are 'embodied' within the action. Again 'embodied' is borrowed from Arnaud Reid (1969). It is useful in that it suggests implicitness.

Whichever kind of attention, aesthetic or functional, is given to the enactment, it requires a special state of consciousness on the part of the participant and the percipient to hold two worlds in mind at the same time, an act of imagination Augusto Boal calls 'metaxis'. This dual consciousness invites in the role-player both submission and detachment. He is able to see his experiencing as an object to be reflected upon. Further than that, like all imaginative states, it can free the individual from his habits of perception and conception. For this reason, I have argued, enactment of any kind, whether functionally or aesthetically attended to, is a powerfully effective tool for the teacher. For education is about change in conception and perception. We must now consider more fully the relationship between drama and learning.

Drama and learning

For the fullest discussion to date on drama and learning the reader should turn to a doctoral thesis by Mike Fleming (1982), Durham University. In the section on learning he is suggesting that changes in views about the nature of the learning process and about education that have occurred during recent years, have placed drama as a medium for learning in an increasingly favourable light. Here I will discuss under two headings firstly the epistemological purpose of drama education, and secondly how learning is achieved.

The epistemological purpose of drama in education

The 'epistemological purpose' sounds grandiose and specious, but I am trying to identify those aspects of drama education which are to do with bringing about change in a participant's understanding of the world as distinct from all the other purposes drama may rightly lay claim to: learning to do drama, learning about drama, learning social skills, learning language skills and learning about oneself (enhancement of self-image, as John Norman calls it). All these purposes are important and in some circumstances any one of them could deserve the teacher's prior attention. In many circumstances the dynamic nature of the medium will guarantee that all these dimensions for change are encompassed within the same work. I accept that teachers who, for instance, are working in circumstances that place *social* learning as a priority will be disappointed that this book offers little direct help (although indirectly the thesis of the book should have considerable implications for social learning).

I am using 'epistemological', therefore, to cover what

148

R. K. Elliott has referred to as the 'breakdown of perceptions and conceptions'. We need to rely on Elliott further, for his views on the main purpose of education are particularly helpful to drama theorists. Elliott's view is that P. Hirst and R. S. Peters (1970) in *The Logic of Education* and other publications have exaggerated the degree to which our mental powers are reflected by or organised by the logic of the seven Forms of Knowledge. He suggests that because their view of the curriculum is based on the erroneous assumption that children's minds will be best developed by being taught all the approved Forms, their recommendations for what should be included in the school curriculum have been at best misleading. Elliott is, of course, but one of many voices now challenging Hirst's theoretical statements on education. Unfortunately, such statements have fortuitously coincided with the reactionary views of examination-minded teachers, university lecturers and politicians who for differing reasons have a vested interest in subject-centred learning.

R. K. Elliott (1975) sees education as the development of mental powers. Understanding is brought about when these mental processes combine with an 'intellectual eros', a composite of energy and desire. The mental powers are not, as Hirst and Peters claim, special to each discipline, but are the basic tools of most intellectual effort. He writes·

> Such powers are exercised, for example, in retention and anticipation; in synthesis and synopsis; in the reduction of whole to parts; in the discernment of relations and discovery of structures; in 'bracketing' properties and aspects; in discovering the objects of feelings and impressions; in guesswork; in pushing ideas to their limits; in shifts of perspective of many kinds; in weighing pros and cons and sensing the balance; and so on (p. 49).

Now it seems to me that the kind of terminology Elliott is using here is very similar to recent drama educationists'

149

attempts to categorise the kind of thinking we want participants to adopt when they are experiencing and reflecting upon their drama.

One of the purposes of drama then can be seen as opportunity to exercise mental powers. But to what end? Elliott (1975) supplies an answer which again echoes the claims of writings in drama education. Elliott is interested in the notion of 'natural' or 'common' understanding, an understanding which is apart from or supersedes the 'bodies of knowledge' of the disciplines, but is itself rigorously disciplined in a unique subjective/objective relationship with the world. It is the kind of understanding that Shakespeare must have had in abundance. It is the kind of understanding most writers whose subject matter is human life have ready access to. It is the kind of understanding we all have to varying degrees and which education could develop if teachers had not chosen to place inordinate faith in subject disciplines: the disciplines should have been used to supplement ordinary understanding not to replace it. In speaking of the man 'educated in the disciplines', Elliott (1975) writes:

> He thinks he has gained from his initiation into the disciplines, whereas in fact he has lost genuineness as a human being (p. 69),

and he argues urgently for the inclusion of education of natural understanding:

> ... there is good reason why education of the natural understanding should be carried on seriously in secondary schools of every type, and a wide variety of courses devised for the purpose, concerning things that matter. It seems a good means of fostering the life of the mind, since the students have to think more for themselves, yet when they express their views would not run immediately into an entanglement of ready-to-hand disciplinary criticism. With good teaching they could penetrate deeply into fields which supposedly belong to the disciplines, and develop points of view of their own

without first having to confront the intimidating power of orthodoxy (p. 66).

It is my view that drama can be one of the most effective ways of developing the 'common understanding'. Its main purpose then can be stated as: *the development of common understanding through the exercise of basic mental powers*, that is, mental powers that are over and above the conventional thinking required of a particular Form of Knowledge.

How learning is achieved

Let us deal first with the more obvious form of drama which I have termed referential or functional, where it is the intention of both teacher and participant to focus attention on some skill or information which is regarded as worthwhile for the participant to acquire. We have already used 'interview technique' as an example of a skill, but in fact many of the 'life-skills' now taught in some of our secondary schools and colleges of F. E. would come under this category. The skill to be learnt may not be as precisely definable as 'interview technique'; it may belong to a category of basic personality traits – self-assertion, for example. These are exercises which give the participant practice in 'being interviewed' or 'having to be more assertive' in order to increase skill in these directions. Sometimes, however, it is *information* rather than skill that is to be given priority and the topics can be as varied as law-court procedures, facts about venereal disease or the different views of child development held by Piaget and Vygotsky.

A feature of referential drama is that the participant usually sees himself as a learner. Now as Mike Fleming has pointed out, this is generally speaking not the case where participants 'create' drama. We can, therefore, now distinguish three characteristics which define role-play as a specific form of enactment: (1) a strong element of simulation, i.e. referring to something in the environment, (2) it involves a generalising abstraction, i.e. it is seen as an instance of a general case, and (3) the participant sees himself as setting out to learn something (or aiding a fellow player to learn something). Having defined role-play in this way let me immediately qualify it by reminding the reader that because of the magic 'as if' the potential for the aesthetic is always present and that, as mentioned in the last chapter, because any kind of enactment requires an initial 'submission' to the experience for it to have any true spontaneity, the participant may 'forget', at least partially, his intention to learn. A good example of the learner's position becoming modified is Harriet Finlay-Johnson's playlet on the Armada (p. 13). It is packed with facts to be learned, but the 'pill' of learning is so sugared by the fun of dramatisation that one wonders whether the pupils perhaps just enjoyed the play-acting.

We are confining our discussion here to epistemological intentions. I am well aware, however, that in some drama or life-skills classes the referential learning outcomes from the role-play exercises can be superseded by other more important achievements to do with group trust, self-esteem, openness to criticism, willingness to discuss with integrity, respect for others' opinions, etc. When this happens, what was supposed to be learnt from the context of the exercise itself fades into the background. It is sometimes the case that the activity of role play continues as a kind of 'front', a protective device that permits a relaxing of normal defences but nevertheless remains securely there as the ostensible task. I am thinking particularly of specialist, small-group work with adolescents and adults.

When we turn to drama proper, as it were, where the intention to create something 'for itself' is uppermost, it is reasonable to ask whether an epistemological view of the drama's content or subject-matter is conceivable. Malcolm Ross (1982) would have it that teachers who see drama in terms of learning are distorting the nature of the art form. He writes:

Aesthetic experience is our experience of the world

transformed by and transfused with love – our love, the love of the beholder or maker. Such experience occasionally reaches the state of rapture and ecstasy as commonly understood. It always implies some degree of standing outside the merely mundane and the sensing in some degree of 'something infinite', of the heart's leaping in wonder as expectation and longing are somehow felt to be satisfied – beyond our dreams and hopes (p. 80).

Reading these words of Ross's makes my attempt to find a theoretical basis for educational drama seem to be some kind of heresy. I am not to be daunted, for I think even Malcolm Ross would concede that art is to do with a way of knowing, and knowing more deeply. It seems to me that an art, in the main, must be dedicated to bringing about change. Either as a maker of art or as a responder to art, I can hope for new insights. And when the art form is *drama*, which draws on the complexities of life directly for its material, it is not unreasonable for me to expect some gain in understanding of life, my life and other people's. What I may be unlikely to be able to do is to explain in propositional terms what form my new insight has taken.

What a teacher has to appreciate is that the children taking part in drama do not set out with an intention to gain new insights, to break habits of conceptions and perceptions. It is in this respect that drama education differs fundamentally from traditional pedagogy. The participant's mental set in entering drama is *not* an 'intention to learn'. It is an intention to create or take part in or solve something. This has two important implications. The first is concerned with the 'personalising' of knowledge and the second with the notion of focus of attention.

(a) Personalising knowledge

The successful outcome of the intention to learn usually includes knowledge of the objective kind – one learns that something is thus either through empirical observation or through a theoretical statement about it. Most knowledge that is transmitted in schools is of the latter kind, a 'received' body of knowledge to be accumulated. Our libraries are full of it. Karl Popper (1972) calls it 'the third world of knowledge' or 'epistemology without a knower'. Now when a learner approaches knowledge of this kind, it is its external form that is the 'given' – and it could be said that whereas the successful learner works from the outside in, making the knowledge his own, the less successful learner works from the outside and stays there! (Both groups can pass examinations!) But when someone comes to know or understand something through his experiencing, his approach to the 'subject-matter' (and here subject-matter becomes the wrong word, for 'experiencing' does not acknowledge the disciplines) is, as it were, from the inside. I wish to claim that what drama does is to create an opportunity for coming to know something *from the inside*, a subjective-objective approach to the material to be understood that is akin to what Kierkegaard meant by knowledge (according to Potjam, 1978) that is both appropriate to the knower and to the thing known.

But the personal knowledge of drama is wrought in a group context. What is individually understood can be socially tested and modified through the medium of public language and action. It is in this sense that drama can be seen as what Iris Murdoch calls a process of 'unselfing', for the group interaction provides a continual counter-pull to subjectivism. In the last chapter we discussed the important break-through from a participant's dramatic playing to a mode of 'presentation', which we saw as a way of objectifying one's private meanings. Ultimately, therefore, drama is concerned with engaging with something outside oneself. The personal aspect of the engagement provides the dynamic, the 'eros' as Elliott calls it, but the orientation is towards objectivity. Only on these grounds can we claim that drama should be at the heart of the curriculum. This orientation, however, will not be achieved if pupils are left to themselves. The teacher carries an enormous responsibility, certain aspects of which will emerge as we look at the second implication of the participant's not functioning as a learner.

(b) Focus of attention

Here again I am grateful to Mike Fleming for directing me towards authors who have brought new thinking to our understanding of the importance of 'unintentional learning'. F. Dunlop (1977) claims that all learning has an essential unintentional component. M. Oakeshott (1967) writes of 'judgement' as a necessary but less than conscious element within the process of acquiring knowledge. D. W. Hamlyn (1973) makes the point that 'coming to see' things in new ways through experience does not imply a conscious attempt to acquire new knowledge. Dunlop writes:

> ... the passive side of learning is itself highly important since a great deal of what is ever learnt is unspecifiable, and hence has to be picked up or acquired at a less than fully conscious level.

This notion of 'passivity' in learning fits with my earlier thesis that entry into a dramatic context is partially 'submissive'. The notion of 'unspecifiability' is in keeping with the lack of definition we have already noted in connection with all 'common knowledge' and with our acknowledgement that a participant in drama may not be able to articulate what he has learnt. All the writers, including, of course, the most well-known exponent of a theory of 'personal knowledge', Michael Polanyi (1958), are interested in the notion of 'tacit' learning or tacit understanding. Mike Fleming writes:

> Now it is one thing to claim that there is a tacit component in learning which must be acknowledged, but it is another matter to suggest that it is the tacit component which is of central importance, which would seem to be the case in most drama work (p. 134).

Polanyi defines two kinds of awareness. He illustrates

them by the classic instance of hammering a nail where both hammer and nail are attended to but each in a different way. The *focal* awareness is on the nail. The *subsidiary* awareness is on the sensations from the handle on the palm of the hand and fingers. The latter sensations 'are not, like the nail, objects of our attention, but instruments of it' (p. 55). Polanyi points out that subsidiary awareness is essential to the carrying out of the task, but if the hammerer started to focus on what his hand is doing instead of on the nail, the equally classic result will obtain! He also uses, appropriately enough, the instance of an actor experiencing stage-fright. If the actor's concentration is on the instrumental means of achieving his role – remembering his lines, saying his words and making gestures with the right quality and clarity of expression, etc., instead of focusing his attention on the *context*, the performance is paralysed. The achievement of a performance lies in a tacit integration of these two levels of awareness.

I wish to suggest there are many more levels of subsidiary awareness for the participant in drama, ranging from what time of day it really is to an anticipation of what someone else in the drama might do next. But most pertinent to this discussion, and just as critical as Polanyi's two levels, is the subsidiary level of aesthetic awareness. The participant, while focusing on the full context of the action and while subsidiarily manipulating his speech and gestures to carry out his actions, may also be giving his attention, at an inner feeling level as opposed to a level of sensation, to the implicit, 'essential' meanings of the context. He may 'sense' the essence of 'motherhood', to use Robert Witkin's example, as he participates in creating an improvisation involving a mother, or as he grapples with Brecht's text of *The Caucasian Chalk Circle*. It is sensed subsidiarily, for it can only be integrated with the whole if his attention is focused on the context and the context in drama means situation, plot or problem to be resolved. If he attempts (or the teacher *requires* him to attempt!) to focus on the aesthetic dimension the enactment will now be paralysed for these rather different reasons.

This has enormous implications for the teacher, for if a pupil is to gain insight into the more significant, universal meanings offered by the aesthetic dimension of the drama experience, not only is it not possible to achieve this deeper level of understanding if from the outset he sees himself functioning as a learner, he will also fail if he attempts to focus his attention directly rather than subsidiarily on the aesthetic dimension. The focus of his attention must be on 'creating a drama' or 'solving a problem'. It is the teacher's focus of attention that must be on the aesthetic dimension while subsidiarily conscious of the importance of the context to the participants.

Here then in drama we have *a unique pedagogic situation*, where a teacher sees himself as teaching but the participant does not see himself as learning; where the teacher focuses on the aesthetic overtones or implications of a context, but the participant focuses on the context; where the teacher looks for opportunities to break the perceptions and conceptions of his pupils but the pupils do not set out with this intention. It is no wonder that Geoff Gillham (1974) coined the phrase, 'A play for the pupil and a play for the teacher', for clearly teacher and pupil are operating on two totally different planes of experiencing. In Chapter Five I wrote of the teacher's skill in terms of structuring; in Chapter Six it centred on judgements about emotional protection. We have emerging in this chapter a skill to do with the teacher's responsibility in integrating these three fundamental levels of awareness: focus on the context; subsidiary awareness of the instrumental means of creating the context; and subsidiary awareness of aesthetic meanings.

One of the interesting features of this way of looking at levels of attention is that in looking at the history of drama in education it appears that the emphasis of the Speech and Drama teachers, because their orientation was towards training, was invariably on the 'instrumental'. Thus a great deal of drama activity reversed the process as described by Polanyi – pupils were to see the 'how' of doing things as the *focus*, and the context as the subsidiary. It was Peter Slade who introduced the notion of *wholeness*, where the context is nearly always to the fore, for the participants are to give their 'whole selves' to the make-believe situation. We now tend to take this approach for granted, but it was one of the aspects of the work that Peter Slade had to fight for. It is one of the important respects in which Dorothy Heathcote identifies with her predecessor Peter Slade. There was a brief period in the 1960s when H.M.I. were making Laban movement fashionable as a form of drama, and the emphasis was placed on training the pupils in the Laban 'thrusts' rather than giving them the chance to move in context. Sometimes today one finds teachers switching sensibly to teach such 'technique' as and when a class seems to require it. Very occasionally one comes across a teacher who automatically assumes that the instrumental level is always the starting point. I recall with some amusement still the teacher who, having read my description of a lesson on the theme of 'Immigration' which started with the 'immigrants' queueing up at a housing office, complained bitterly that I had failed to introduce them to the subject by getting them to 'move like immigrants'!

Nevertheless, there *are* times when a teacher may deliberately focus on this subsidiary, practical level. When I was working with a group of enthusiastic but apprehensive teachers in Reykjavik we were to dramatise Iceland's dependency on the sea. The incident was a ship-wreck, but in order to 'protect' I approached the topic in a way that was both indirect and projected: the participants were to be the women waiting at the quayside for the men whose boat did not appear on the horizon. Now I knew it was no use setting up a freely structured interaction; the group was not ready to have any kind of context as the focus of their attention. I began with each woman on her own doing a technical mime exercise of sewing a patch on a pair of trousers (the period was nineteenth century). What a protective exercise this proved to be, for embarrassed participants found they could legitimately keep their eyes down! Given the security of this technical practice we then moved it 'into context' – a context of women waiting, women whose fingers are busy as they wait. *Now* they have the courage to 'look out to sea', comforted by the thought that they can revert to the subsidiary practical level if their embarrassment overtakes them again.

Now this example of projection can be multiplied by instances from work with children. I recall working with a class of fourteen-year-old girls who wanted to be 'in a mad-house', so I started with 'the problem of tying one's shoe-lace when concentration is not high'; ten-year-olds who were to be detectives practised pretending to read a newspaper while watching someone; nine-year-olds practised marching properly in order to be guards; sixteen-year-olds as old people began by finding out whether age had affected their handwriting; five-year-olds who had to creep up on a giant to steal his keys practised 'creeping without a sound'. These are obvious well-worn teacher 'exercises' that occasionally come in handy when there is a good reason for delaying entry with their 'whole selves' into a context.

What is less obvious from this list is the level of teacher's thinking. He knows that these preliminary 'technical' activities are to be superseded as soon as possible by action 'in context', but in context to the children often means plot, getting on with a sequence of events, or solving a problem – 'the play for the pupils', as Geoff Gillham has called it. The teacher's focus of attention, however, must be along aesthetic dimensions. Unless the class is experienced enough in drama to do it for themselves, he must find opportunities to inject 'indications' which may, *at a subsidiary level of consciousness*, be picked up by the participants whose focal attention is necessarily on the task or plot. Thus the initial choice of 'sewing a patch on trousers' as an exercise is not an arbitrary one. For the *teacher* this has symbolic overtones to do with the themes of 'waiting', of 'the irony of continuing to patch the clothing of the man who will not return', of 'the intimacy of a husband/wife relationship', of 'the place and duty of a nineteenth-century wife', of 'submission to the dictates of the sea', of 'the women of a community grouped together in tragedy', etc. This is not to say that a teacher in setting up this particular exercise makes a list of possible universal meanings. It is much more likely that a choice feels *intuitively* right (for the teacher is working from within the art form, not intellectually from the outside) and that after the event he is able to intellectualise about the usefulness of his choice. Now the participants themselves may or may not become aware of those same aesthetic dimensions. Some may respond to meanings far beyond anything the teacher could have foreseen, meanings that can never be articulated. And when this does occur there is a chance that previous perceptions and conceptions become eroded and new insights are felt.

Change in understanding at this sub-conscious level is a *felt* change. It may be possible to give it a partial articulation: when a woman says, 'My son will wear these trousers when he goes to sea; one can only guess at what her new understanding might be. And sometimes the change of feeling is wrought at a still deeper level when it is a strong sense of *form* (the silence of a group of women whose eyes keep watch on the sea, the tension of a kind of timelessness) that stirs one's feelings. We are near here to what I think Robert Witkin means when he talks of the relationship within an event, that is, its deep structure that arouses tensions within us that can only be expressed through the medium of another art form.

A response at this depth of feeling is not, of course, the prerogative of drama; all the arts are capable of touching people deeply. But drama happens to be one of the arts to which the response is shared by members of a group, as it is in dancing and music-making. It was demonstrated in the last chapter that the dramatic-playing/performance mode is a dialectical relationship sometimes emphasising one rather than the other. When the actors set out to 'represent' to an audience they are

160

using dramatic art in its theatre form; when the participants have no audience and no sense of rehearsing 'ready for an audience' they are sharing their creation with each other. *Both* can be art of the highest kind. For drama is both a performance and a *communal* art.

This brings me to a point where I need to redress the balance of this book. I have in the last three chapters attempted an analysis of drama pedagogy. What has emerged is drama's double valence towards the artistic and the 'functional', that is, its *usefulness* as a means of teaching about life. This separates it from the other arts in a way which, of course, other educationalists with a vested interest in the arts do not always wish to acknowledge (see, for instance, the Gulbenkian report (1982) which totally ignores the pedagogic aspect of drama in its anxiety to find 'sameness' in the arts). It also puts drama in a unique relationship with the rest of the curriculum, for there is a sense in which the rest of the curriculum is drama's subject-matter, particularly at a level of values, issues and implications. Any book of this kind, therefore, must emphasise drama as a medium for education at all levels and in all directions. But this is to ignore the 'other face' of drama: *drama as celebration*. Drama, it seems to me, is *not* always about change in understanding. It is also about celebrating a community's existence. In Chapter Five I wrote about drama as a 'game', choosing to concentrate on what that implies *structurally*, but drama is linked with game in the much broader, anthropological sense. Games, festivals and rituals are not about change but about a collective identity. The 'other face' of drama shares this communal purpose. This is what a school play can be about – not *should* but *can* be about. Some school play performances, however, impressively continue to use theatre in its more dynamic sense where young people are given the chance to make their own theatre about things that matter to them, what David Self (1978) calls 'creative theatre'. This is an extension of classroom work which is to be admired and encouraged. Nevertheless, having significance of quite a different kind is the annual school play or school musical that is put on to celebrate the school's existence as a community – although one rarely hears it spoken of in these terms. There are few occasions in a school's life that give pupils and staff together such a strong, shared sense of well-being

Extending this point, there is a particular need in our television-bound society to employ new ways of re-finding a communal identity. Community theatre in this country is not new; as we have seen in Chapter Four in the recent past it has had considerable influence on the drama scene. One of the reasons this influence faded, however, was that as more emphasis was placed on *training*, less and less was placed on having something important to say. Although I have spoken of theatre as a celebration of the status quo, and indeed have gone so far as to suggest that a school production that is no more than that has nothing of which to be ashamed, adult community theatre needs a more significant dynamic.

Summary

Enactment – a special state of consciousness

In this chapter I have attempted to identify qualities and levels of consciousness that appear to obtain during the practice of dramatic activity:

(1) *Metaxis*, holding two worlds in mind at the same time, is the central dynamic of the imaginative act.

(2) It permits an increased capacity for detachment from the experiencing: what is submitted to passively is also actively construed and reflected upon.

(3) That it is expressed in concrete action brings about the magic 'as if', a responding to a presence that in reality is absent.

(4) This creates the double valence of dramatic action – it is open to either aesthetic or literal attention. The latter is referential in meaning; the former is 'essential' or universal in meaning.

(5) Both 'intentions of mind' can bring about change in perception and conception, although the latter is more

likely to be at a 'felt' level of consciousness than the former.

(6) The focus of attention in drama is desirably on the *context* to which the participant brings his 'whole self'. *Subsidiarily*, he must be technically aware of how he is creating the context *and* if the creation is to be significant, he must also be aware of aesthetic dimensions either at a level that can be partially articulated or as deeply felt tensions sensed within the form itself.

(7) Any change in understanding is likely to take place at a lower than conscious level, giving support to Brian Way's notion of the importance of 'relishing and enjoying, irrespective of whether there is full understanding'.

(8) Although the relationship between the participant and the point of reference is a subjective/objective one, the overall mental orientation from within the drama is towards objectivity.

(9) Because it is a group enterprise, there is a natural striving towards 'finding a public voice', towards having one's feelings and thoughts publicly tested, towards collaborative meaning.

Drama and pedagogy

The purpose of drama education is to develop the powers of the mind so that a 'common' understanding of life can be mastered. Common understanding cuts across the 'forms' of knowledge and is a rigorous way of approaching school subjects from the 'inside', rather than from the more normal view of a subject as a collection of 'given' knowledge. But this approach to pedagogy is unconventional for the learner does not and, indeed, should not see himself in that role. This puts an enormous responsibility on the teacher, far more than any previous history of drama in education has expected. It is the teacher who has to structure for change in perception and conception. It is also the teacher who has to focus on aesthetic potential if the participants themselves seem only to be operating at a literal level.

Drama as art

Drama can be either a shared group experience or a theatrical performance: both can achieve artistic endeavour. In placing a great deal of emphasis on pedagogy, as a book of this kind is bound to do, the alternative view of drama may become neglected. This is the view of drama as celebration of a communal identity. The school play may well be seen in this light. What has in recent years been lost to us as Community Drama, so flourishing in the 1950s, should be revived, but in the more dynamic form of theatre as challenge to the status quo.

8 In context

In this, the final chapter, I wish to move forward simultaneously on a number of fronts. I shall once more pick up the historical thread which has been running through the book. I shall attempt to reinforce the usage of some of the terms introduced in the last three chapters, particularly those of 'indirectness' and 'projection'. 'Mantle of the Expert' will be examined as a dramatic phenomenon uniquely adaptive to educational ends. We have seen that a number of assumptions related to the nature of drama, of education, of knowledge, of children and of the responsibility of the teacher are implicit in the work of the educational pioneers. In this chapter I shall focus on assumptions about 'context' for not only does this emerge as a key concept in making comparisons of different pioneers, it seems also to point the way to a more sophisticated understanding of the relationship between drama and learning.

By 'in context' we mean interaction within a dramatic event. The participants, adopting a mental disposition of *metaxis*, agree to behave *as if* they are sharing the same fiction. It is characterised by its immediacy. If the words are 'given' beforehand, as in a scripted play, then the immediacy is necessarily simulated. Both forms of behaviour, the spontaneous interaction and the performance projected through the printed word qualify as contextual. In respect of 'context', Harriet Finlay-Johnson, Caldwell Cook, the Community Drama exponents, Peter Slade and Dorothy Heathcote have much in common. For each of them, creating a dramatic context was central to their work. This would have been to state the obvious had it not been that the most influential pioneer of all, Brian Way, weaned teachers away from the dramatic context.

Drama as Education

There was a precedent for this in that the Speech and Drama experts of the 1940s and 1950s tended to turn increasingly to speech and mime exercises with the focus, as we indicated in the last chapter, on the instrumental rather than the contextual. Brian Way, following Stanislavsky's early writings about his training of actors, sought material that gave pupils practice in concentration, sensitivity and imagination, material which tended to eschew the complexity of the dramatic event. Now the effect on teachers and curriculum planners has been quite extraordinary for in some parts of the world whole curricula have been drawn up on the principle of avoiding dramatic contexts.

Because in England our schools have never placed a great deal of faith in writing up and keeping to detailed syllabuses, especially in the arts and humanities subjects, it often only emerges from observation of classroom practice what any particular teacher's philosophy might be. It is difficult therefore to identify any kind of trend, but in a country where the state *requires* a detailed submission of intentions, philosophies are laid out in black and white. It was only in my recent visit abroad, when I was invited to read various graded syllabuses in drama, that it hit me between the eyes the extent to which the notion of avoiding any significant drama context, in favour of direct training in life-skills, was having a suffocating effect on the content of drama lessons in schools. There was a logic, though in my view ill-founded, in what the perpetrators claimed. They had recognised that in the past their concept of drama for school students as Theatre Arts with a heavy emphasis on acting training was leading to very superficial work. However, instead of asking themselves, 'Are there therefore other approaches to drama available?', they worked on the assumption that what was needed was a pre-training programme which would give students resources for life and which would be useful to any who at a more mature age would take up acting. Effectively the baby has been thrown out with the bath water – and experienced drama teachers are at a loss to

166

know what they are doing, allowing their own skills to atrophy.

Thus it is important that we see this discussion of drama 'in context' against a popular trend of taking drama *out* of context or, more accurately, *without* a context. Dorothy Heathcote's early pioneering work sought to bring the dramatic content back into the drama lesson. Like Peter Slade she sought ways of setting up drama that required pupils to bring their 'whole selves' into the dramatic event. It was at this time she coined the phrase 'living through', implying a spontaneous interaction within the dramatic situation using a dramatic playing orientation. But whereas in the main Slade was keen to see the created content as a vehicle for the pupils' subjective expression, Heathcote saw the subject-matter or content of the created context to be as worthy of objective attention as any play written for the theatre. Her favourite catch-phrase in the 1960s, making a parallel with Kenneth Tynan's (1957) view of theatre, was that drama is about 'A man in a mess'. This might have successfully drawn teachers' attention to the importance of content, but it inadvertently led teachers into two distinct but related traps. One is what might be called the 'crisis' trap; the other the 'literal' trap.

Teachers would regularly look around for what new 'mess' they could put their classes into and, encouraged by their pupils' choices, they would flit from one catastrophe to another. One could almost hear their planning as: 'Well, we've now done Drowning, Mountain Rescue and Famine ... what should we go on to next? Fire, perhaps?' Malcolm Ross (1982) is right to have misgivings about the kinds of topic that are popularly chosen in drama, for they invite both teachers and pupils to fall headlong into the trap of expecting the dramatic context to carry the simulation of huge catastrophes, the dimensions of which cannot be sustained by the limited psychological resources of most pupils.

The second trap is to perceive the dramatic event as literal, as important in itself instead of as a lens through

which to search beyond the event to its social, anthropological, historical or aesthetic implications. For Dorothy
Heathcote the key word in the phrase 'A man in a mess'
is not *mess* but *man*, for drama illuminates our understanding of mankind. The particularity of the event is a
lens, not a mirror. Extending this metaphor further it is
possible to describe Dorothy's work in recent years as
'prismatic'. It is as if she has said to herself, 'What do you
see if, instead of looking directly through a lens, you use
a second lens with which to look through the first lens?'
This 'prismatic' device is not new. In the theatre we watch
the murder of Hamlet's father – but not directly – through
the analogue of a play performed by hired actors – but
not directly – for we are watching Claudius watching
. . . etc. In the *Marat/Sade* we look at the French Revolution from the perspective of an asylum for the insane.
In Peter Brook's *A Midsummer Night's Dream* we catch the
Elizabethan's awe of magic *through* our own sense of
wonder at the conjurer's unearthly skill. Returning to
drama in education, we have already referred to the
example from Chris Lawrence's teaching in which with
a class of juniors a close study of selected animals in
London Zoo was channelled through the task of helping
a group of actors to represent those animals in movement
form. The pupils had to re-focus their newly acquired
knowledge of the animals in terms of what they understood of the dance form and of the limitations of the
artistes' personalities and skills.

Now this 'prismatic' structure to drama – or to use
Dorothy's metaphor drawn from Goffman (1975),
'framing' – brings a new complexity to our understanding
of 'context', which I have defined above as interaction,
spontaneous or scripted within a fictitious situation.
Improvising a 'war' situation and performing scenes from
Oh What a Lovely War would both qualify as 'context'.
Both utilise a dramatic present and presence in order to
create meanings relevant to the topic of war. Conversely,
activities in the drama lesson that did not require the
participants to adopt an 'as if' mental set could be desig-

nated as 'out of context'. There are, however, two distinct kinds of 'out of context' – for example, *reflecting* on a context through discussion compared with, say, relaxation exercises. The categories could therefore be more sensibly designated: 'in context', 'out of context', and 'no context'. Much activity based on Brian Way's approach to drama could be placed in the last category. A close examination of Dorothy Heathcote's early teaching reveals that most of the activity was of the first kind, an inter-action within the fiction, but nevertheless punctuated by a breaking 'out of context' in order to reflect on the work. (Indeed, reflection on experience has always been of prime importance for Dorothy.) What she has done in recent years, however, is to blur the edges between 'in' and 'out' of context.

In Chapter Six I introduced the notion of 'protecting into emotion', suggesting that the two most effective ways of doing this are by using indirectness and projection. Both of these structural devices (and 'frame' is a particu-larly effective form of indirectness) challenge the simplicity of context as we have so far understood it. Both tend to take the participants to the 'edge' of the context, for Dorothy has discovered it is often the case that approaching a topic from the edge allows for a state of mind that is *both* reflective and engaged. She believes that endowing pupils with the role responsibility of historians looking at a reproduction of Picasso's *Guernica* has a greater chance of helping them to find new understanding about the violence of war than if the drama involved them in appropriate simulated acts of aggression. And yet, of course, the latter would look like proper drama, whereas the former may not appear to be a dramatic context at all. Paradoxically, while reacting strongly against the 'no context' approach of Brian Way, Dorothy Heathcote has evolved a way of working that on the surface appears to be even less dramatic. It is no wonder that people like Margaret Faulkes Jendyk (1975), echoing what many of us in the 1950s asked of Samuel Beckett's plays when they first arrived on the West End stage, ask 'Is this

169

drama?' Dorothy has changed the *appearance* of a drama lesson to such an extent that many people who watch her at work feel bewildered and frustrated because the criteria they would normally apply seem to be redundant.

But the *centre* of Dorothy's work is essentially 'in context', the 'as if' frame often being so sketchily drawn that one can hardly recognise it. Such sketchiness is not casualness. For instance, early in the session on the Bronze Age which we shall be examining later in this chapter in some detail, the pupils are invited to draw images they associated with Bronze Age People. They look at each others' drawings as they work on the floor. 'Let's put them up on the wall, as if in a gallery . . .' Dorothy suggests. They do this and proceed to walk round the walls. The 'as if in a gallery' gives a slight but significantly different perspective to the looking – and *drama has started*. The pupils' behaviour may not outwardly be affected; certainly no passer-by is going to perceive a drama lesson going on; but the opportunity for *metaxis*, the special state of mind that permits them to see a 'gallery' wall instead of a classroom wall and a 'gallery' space instead of a classroom space has been 'casually' offered by the teacher. From where they are on the very edge of the context, the pupils can painlessly, imperceptibly, move out of context or nearer to the centre as the occasion demands.

But in changing the outward appearance of the drama in this way, Dorothy has challenged an earlier assumption which seemed up to now to be incontrovertible. When in the 1960s she was talking about 'living through', she was, as we have seen, giving support to Peter Slade's concept of personal play. The distinction Slade drew between activities such as sport and drama which demand the 'whole selves', a total physical/emotional/intellectual engagement, and activities such as Maths, Reading, crafts and painting which demand the 'projected' self, i.e. one's energies focused *through* the object of attention, seemed both valid and useful. Slade argued that in education a child should be given a balanced diet of personal and projected play, that many immature adults are people who were deprived of personal play. Child Drama is personal play par excellence.

In recent years Dorothy Heathcote has turned this distinction on its head. Whereas Slade valued projected play, he saw its connection to drama in activities such as directing plays, making model theatres and manipulating puppets. Dorothy now employs a structure that brings these contrasted use of energies within the same experience. I have suggested in the paragraph above that an important feature of her work is that it often lies at the edge of a context, facilitating movement further in or out, but an important dynamic of her work is also that the 'living through' (as she has called it, or personal play as Slade describes it, or dramatic playing, to use my own terminology) remains *partial*, modified by its opposite, a projection through a task which in turn is tempered by the pull towards dramatic playing. The activity of looking at the Bronze Age drawings on the wall, a distinctly projected activity, is heightened by the dramatic playing context of 'as if we were in a gallery'.

We shall see that the organising structures of Dorothy's Bronze Age sessions are complex. Let us first, therefore, use an illustration with which we are already familiar (see page 82 for the 'Way West' project by Cecily O'Neill and Alan Lambert). In Chapter Five I attempted an analysis of certain steps within the sequence in terms of 'game' structures, which allowed us to look at the 'internal' event. We will now take a second examination, but this time from the point of view of context, projection, directness (including 'frame') and presentation. We shall also be able to note the *sequences* of experiences in terms of how the above elements are juxtaposed.

'The Way West' (from *Drama Structures* by Cecily O'Neill and Alan Lambert)

(1) The teacher shows a genuine photograph of a group of people who travelled together on the Oregon Trail.

(This is 'out of context' requiring passive projection; dealing directly with the topic.)

(2) She holds a discussion on why people might choose to undertake the dangerous journey.

(This is 'out of context'; active in potential; but because it has switched from 'these are the people who went' to the less direct 'reasons for going' it can be described as indirect.)

(3) In pairs one partner assumes the role of any one of the people in the photograph and tells the other (a colleague, friend or relative) why he is tempted to go on the journey.

(This is 'in context'; exercise form – dramatic playing in mode rather than performance; indirect.)

(4) Class together again – the second partners report to the rest of the class what they have heard.

(This is 'out of context'; indirect; active, requiring a 'presentational' (i.e. public) form.)

(5) Teacher-in-role starts a class improvisation as if they were a local community in the Mid-West hearing what a bright future they might have if only they would abandon homes and move West.

(This is 'in context'; at first: projected and passive – participants are merely experiencing through the teacher's role. As the scene gathers momentum it switches to active dramatic playing; indirect, in so far as it continues to deal with the preliminaries to the main event.)

The above sequence varies the experiences while retaining a logical coherence in terms of subject-matter and is evenly 'protective' throughout. The only time this protection is removed is in 4, which although 'out of context' carries 'public' status. Notice that virtually the whole session deals with the 'decision to go' and does not plunge into the event itself.

It is interesting to compare and contrast the 'Way West'

with another series of lessons referred to in Chapter Five – the 'Mystery Pictures' (see pages 96). Here again the topic is dealt with entirely indirectly in the sense that at no point are the participants required to *experience* the mysterious incident through direct interaction. They do apply their minds to the topic, but this time distanced by *retrospect* (in contrast to the 'Way West' which *anticipated*) and by the use of *frame*, for the pupils are in role as medical staff looking at a patient's dilemma – and at first they do not meet the patient, only the drawings. Thus we have an instance of nicely balancing personal and projected play; while they are in role as doctors, in a dramatic playing context, their attention and therefore their energies are projected through the drawings. Their behaviour in role as doctors is in fact controlled and seriously modified by the constrictions of viewing the drawings.

Let us turn now to the sequence of sessions by Dorothy Heathcote on the Bronze Age. I am grateful to Phyl Herbert, a student of Dorothy's, who for her Master's dissertation made a detailed study of Dorothy's project in order to evolve an epistemological rationale for the 'Mantle of the Expert'. I cannot do justice to this excellent dissertation for my purpose here is but to itemise the sequence of events in order to demonstrate the convoluted structures Dorothy employed in order to teach some young adolescents about the Bronze Age period. The reader must bear in mind that for my purpose I am only offering the skeletal framework of the lessons.

The Bronze Age
Phase 1 On the blackboard is written:

Pupils are invited to conjure up images of things and to say what they saw.

(This appears to be a similar beginning to 'Way West'

in that it is out of context and projected, but in fact it is significantly different. Cecily O'Neill is presenting her class with an obvious 'drama' situation – people who have to make an enormous decision about their lives, 'a man in a mess' epitomised. But Dorothy is in a different game altogether. To have this early phase of work on the Bronze Age cluttered with people with problems would have been crude hyperbole. All that she offers them is a phrase on a blackboard, uncompromising in its starkness. Cecily was right to start with an authentic photograph to help the pupils start with their dramatic adventure. Equally, in working in 'Mantle of the Expert' Dorothy was right to make authenticity something her pupils were going to have to work for – step by painful step, if necessary. And to begin with, the Bronze Age is going to be a world of things, not people at all.)

Phase 2 They are invited to draw the objects they had in their mind.

(This is out of context; indirect, in the sense of not dealing directly with a Bronze Age *event*; projected, active.)

Phase 3 They are invited to look round at others' drawings.

(This is out of context; projected (passive, for they do not take the chance offered to ask questions or make comments); indirect.)

Phase 4 Labelling their own drawings ... 'Label the parts of the picture that correspond to "I know this"; "I think this"; or "I wonder about this".'

(This is out of context; indirect; projected (intellectually active).)

Phase 5 Pupils invited to stick drawings on wall, 'as if' for a gallery, and to move around 'as if' *in* a gallery.

(This is in context; indirect; projected; dramatic playing; beginnings of frame, i.e. there is just a hint of their beginning to be expert onlookers.)

Phase 6 Dorothy uses 'time machine' metaphor with class to invite them now to be 'visiting' a Bronze Age

Community. She uses six adults draped in black with stone coloured masks to enter the space to represent monoliths from the past. The class observes in silence. The teacher then asks, 'What *did* you see going on?'

This simple device is in fact fascinatingly complex, for teacher has removed the class into another dramatic context, or rather, theatrical context, for they are spectators to a theatrical statement – but, not quite, for they are sharing the same space as the 'actors'. As long as the pupils remain passive observers they can safely continue to project their attention onto the 'stones' just as the infants projected their attention onto me as a witch referred to in Chapter Six. If the teacher at this point makes the mistake of expecting the pupils to interact either with the stones or with each other, thus removing the protection of projection (as I did in the 'witch' lesson when I sensed the infants were ready to cope with dramatic playing without projection), the work would no doubt have collapsed. Dorothy has given them a flavour of *directness* (actually to be there, the Bronze Age, in the present and *presence* evoked through the symbols of the stones, but quickly and abruptly she changes to the past tense, 'What *did* you see?' – back to indirect reporting).

Phase 7 Dorothy now contrives an elaborate expertise role for the pupils: they are to be administrators of a Bronze Age Community Project. She imposes the notion on them that some part of the British Isles environment is to be set aside as a genuinely functioning *simulated* Bronze Age in which volunteers will actually live for six years. This and subsequent steps represent different ways into this particular expertise. This is the first move she has made explicitly to endow the pupils with roles. They are presented with application forms from likely and unlikely candidates who wish to be considered for the six-year venture. Elaborate discussions of a particular applicant's worthiness are held between teacher and pupils in role.

(It is here that I would prefer to change the metaphor to

175

'prism', for this is a good example of double, if not treble 'framing'. Not only is there the 'expertise' frame, but the Bronze Age itself is to be 'framed' for it is to be seen through the perspective of a modern environment being adapted to the requirements of simulation. Additionally, the first angle of approach is through the applications, so that the participants' initial attention is directed towards the kind of background that can be gleaned from reading between the lines of letters and forms of application. It's not just a prism – it's a bloody Hall of Mirrors!

In Summary – in context; indirect; frame-in-a-frame or prismatic; active; projected.)

Phase 8   The 'experts' are to select a site, using a map of the British Isles.

(It is in context; indirect; prismatic; active.)

Phase 9   They now place the 'stones' (adults dressed up) 'as if' dealing with the real environment.

(This is in context; indirect (as far as topic of Bronze Age) but direct (as far as setting up a site); projected, in that they are directing where the adults should stand, looking from the outside as it were; active.)

Phase 10   An encounter with teacher-in-role as representative from Army with shooting rights in the vicinity and as a farmer from whom land is to be rented.

(This is a completely different dynamic from anything that's gone before. It is in context; both direct and indirect (as for Phase 9); non-projected dramatic playing; active.)

Phase 11   Inspecting and measuring site.

(This is another example of those 'search' games referred to in Chapter Five which can only be real when the capacity for appropriate mental imagery is high. With all the preceding ten phases behind them presumably the class now had these resources.

In context; direct and indirect; on the border-line between projected and non-projected.)

Phase 12   They are to put their 'findings' on maps of the site.

(This is in context; prismatic; projected; active.)

Phase 13   The class now split into smaller groups each led by a 'stone' and each group further divided between 'experts of modern times making a simulated site' and 'real Bronze Age people' (notice this is the first time this kind of role has been required) who are going to advise them what to do. The pupils combine the miming of tasks that are set out for the experts in professional looking files with the drawing of implements they are using.

(This is now indirect and framed for the 'moderns' and direct for the 'Bronze Age people'; active and projected through the files and drawings, but non-projected dramatic playing for the interactions.)

Phase 14   The 'stones' are now to elevate the pupils' work into a demonstration of tasks that both communities, the modern and the ancient combine to perform. As each 'stone' narrates in turn each group mimes the tasks, to the watching audience.

(This is the first use of performance mode, the narrator elevating the status of the pupils' actions. Notice how this performance is both exposing because it is public but also protective because of the formality. In summary it is in context; direct; active and passive (according to whether actor or spectator); and, similarly, non-projected and projected. This marks the end of the Mantle of the Expert approach.)

Phase 15   Dorothy now feels the class are ready to switch to a 'man in a mess' experiential drama. Notice it has taken fourteen steps to reach a point which for many teachers would be a starting point! She is going to introduce the notion of a Bronze Age community meeting a crisis and invites them to make suggestions, arising from their tasks, about what might go wrong for their community. (*Notice* – what might go wrong for their *community*; if it is decided someone is to be taken seriously ill, for example, then the drama will focus on how this affects the order of things in the society.)

In order to help them visualise how to set up a crisis

drama, she uses a 'depiction' of a 'man with a sore hand' who fails to melt the copper and tin needed by the community. Dorothy goes to the extent of marking a 'bruise' on a pupil's hand so that the idea is given a concrete image.

(Here Dorothy is teaching about how drama works – by finding a concrete image to act as a microcosm of imminent disaster. This is the first instance recorded in Phyl Herbert's account of *direct teaching*. All the teaching so far, which, of course, I have omitted in the above notes, has been done obliquely through role or innuendo or running commentary. For this demonstration the pupils are momentarily: out of context; passive; projecting.)

Phase 16 A lengthy discussion takes place, with teacher trying to abdicate responsibility, about what kind of crisis they would like. They eventually choose 'Fire'.

(This is the first time the class has been thrown onto its own resources as a group. Dorothy recognises, I am sure, at this point that unless they can cope with the problem of making a decision about a topic, their group dynamics may well interfere with their ability to carry out the crisis drama. So she tries to teach them about themselves, very subtly trying to make them aware of what is happening to them as they argue among themselves. This, importantly, is out of context; non-projected; a face to face encounter, with leaders emerging.)

Phase 17 Phase 17 should really be split up into six further phases for Dorothy stops the preparation work on the crisis six times – and they never actually experience the 'fire'. She will not allow anything less than truthfulness. She is working along two main dimensions. The first is in respect of the particularity of the events – and any lack of belief she will not tolerate; the second relates to the implications of the community's responsibility, for 'a man in a mess' is *not* about the mess. A drama about a fire is of little value if that is all it is about. The fire is the lens through which a society's culture may be understood. If the pupils fail on the first they will not get anywhere near the second – and the experience becomes educationally invalid. It is a better learning experience if the pupils go through the frustrations of not quite pulling it off, than if they are allowed to deceive themselves that the 'fire' drama has been real. In fact in this final stage of Dorothy's work with the class the 'fire' is never created – except in their anticipations. To the pupils it must have seemed to be unfinished, which again points to another important aspect of Dorothy's philosophy: for her no drama is ever finished. It is always a new starting.

This is the only aspect of the 12 hours' work that gets anywhere near a fully contextual, direct, unframed, non-projected, 'living through' experience. They are in role as Bronze Age people doing Bronze Age things dramatically playing a sequence about a fire. Ironically, however, the intensity or integrity of dramatic playing was hardly achieved, for Dorothy's attempts to hand over the power to the participants was undermined by their lack of persistence in aiming for truthfulness. It is interesting to note that during the final phases of the 'Mantle of the Expert' approach the pupils were taking on responsibility for their own work, but simulating a crisis demanded a group identification and a *directness* of interaction they were not ready for. Thus the apparent dramatic playing became modified almost out of existence: Dorothy had to keep re-taking the power to such an extent that their experience was virtually becoming a projected one, projected through teacher's own use of role. Their unreadiness seems a likely cause but another kind of explanation seems possible. In Chapter Five, I discussed the importance of dramatic playing having an internal 'game' structure. This seems to have been lacking in the way Dorothy set it up. It is possible she over-estimated the degree to which the tension of having something precious (a community's wealth) destroyed would be real for them as it was for her. I do not think this point will worry Dorothy unduly as she may be satisfied that the important learning took place in the process of *preparing* for the 'fire'.

The reader of the above description of a series of sessions on the Bronze Age must not conclude that it presents some kind of model to be followed step by step. I have included it as a way of conveying the wide range of strategies and contexts that are available to any teacher in the process of planning a sustained piece of work. The sequence, while interesting and illuminating, is not there to be rigidly followed. Nor is the work to be seen as a series of steps towards dramatic playing in context. Dorothy just happened to conclude it with this kind of interaction, but the work could have stopped at Phase 14, for that was a kind of completion point for the 'Mantle of the Expert' approach. Nor should this lengthy description be taken as a strong recommendation from me that 'Mantle of the Expert' is always the best approach. I am more interested in demonstrating the vast permutations that are available than that a teacher should follow a particular style. In order to counter-balance the above analysis, therefore, I now propose to give the outline of a plan for one lesson, a lesson whose elegant structure does not use 'Mantle of the Expert'. It is the work of a group of P.G.C.E. Drama students from Birmingham Polytechnic (1981–82) who, towards the end of their course, gave themselves the challenge of trying to prepare a drama experience with a class of young adolescents on a delicate topic, a topic which had actually come from one particular class of pupils on the students' school practice. They use a narrative form for their planning, making it more easily readable. (Certainly the reader will find it much easier to follow than my analysis above!)

'Rape' lesson

The following comprises a prepared lesson on rape for a third-year class.

The class decided at the end of the last lesson that they wished to do a lesson on rape. The teacher, knowing the class fairly well, assesses that the suggestion is sincere and not just an attempt to put the teacher on the spot.

The teacher realises at the planning stage that even though the class has asked for a lesson on rape, they are too young and inexperienced to tackle the subject in a direct manner but will need to have this element of the drama 'referred to' (as in the manner of a Greek drama).

She also realises that the girl the class nominated as the 'victim' must be protected from any stigma that *could* be implied by the role. (The nominee is a popular girl who is fairly well-developed and is not unwilling to take on the role.)

She considers aspects of the chosen subject to find which might be the key to the learning from a lesson with this age group and decides that the stereotyping of women and the resultant lack of freedom are both implicit in the subject. From this she decides that her key question could be: 'Why should girls have less freedom than boys?'

She has now to balance on the one hand the feelings of the girl who was nominated for the part against the rather stereotyped reactions of many who would say that a victim of rape 'asked for it'. So her next concern is to ensure that the class must have some sort of 'invest-ment' in the character that the girl will play, even though they *may* be expecting a vicarious thrill.

The Lesson
The class through questioning build up a picture of the girl – she's popular – why? The class re-enact a few incidents to illustrate why the girl is popular: The time the girl stood up to an older kid who was bullying her friend. The time she gave her only ticket to see 'Madness' live at a local concert to a friend who had recently recovered from a road accident and therefore couldn't get a ticket for her favourite group, etc. One of these illustrations is set in a Youth Club.

181

(The main part of the lesson plan hinges upon the activities in a Youth Club and in this case is used for the rest of the drama. If this had not occurred, teacher would have introduced this location.)

The Youth Club setting used by one group is used again for the next part of the drama and is quite good in that it is a place where boys and girls meet in a situation that is both informal and with which the class can identify in terms of role.

The teacher feeds in some information – they are all members of a Youth Club and there is to be an inter-Youth Club Beauty Competition. The class decide that the prize should be that a local, popular band will play a gig at the club from which the chosen Beauty Queen is a member. The girl volunteer is to be their entrant.

The class discuss what she should wear for the competition – 'A short skirt and sexy top' says one lad. 'No, high heels and a long dress,' says a girl, 'like on Miss World', and friends offer to loan clothes. The group decide she should wear a short skirt and top. The sister of one of the girls is a hairdresser who can fix her hair and one of the boys says he'll get his brother to pick her up and take her to the competition hall a few miles away in his car. In this way she'll not mess up her hair or outfit. They decide that she should wear some make-up, 'but not too much', and that they'll have a dress rehearsal that night. The girl practises her walk, 'don't forget to smile', says one of the girls, while one of the boys acts as compere asking questions of her 'like they do in beauty competitions'.

(At this point the class investment in the girl is high, they have given her help in many different ways so that she is, in their eyes, capable of winning. The prize that they decided upon is obviously one which they would like to enjoy and a good majority of the class will now feel that they cannot lose.)

At this point the teacher stops the drama and asks them to get out of the costume cupboard (well stocked) something that they feel would match the verbal description of the clothes they have decided their volunteer should wear. The teacher takes these and shows them to the class.

The teacher narrates the next section of the drama: The girl came second in the competition, feeling she had let down her friends after all the help they had given her she runs off before they can talk to her. The class objects, 'She's daft doing that, we don't mind.'

'It's not her fault the judge needed glasses.' They decide to go back and have a party at the Youth Club '. . . after all, she did come second.'

For the following section the teacher asks that they place their chairs formally as if they are in assembly at school. (While they are doing this she places the clothes of the girl into a brown paper bag.) She then tells them that the members of the Youth Club are all pupils at the same school and that it is the following day. They have been called together at a special meeting so that the Headmistress can speak to them. She asks them to react to the entrance of the Head in the usual manner.

The Headmistress walks in, stands in front of the assembled class and in a grave, quiet voice asks them to sit down. Continuing in this tone, 'Something rather dreadful has happened . . .' she goes on to inform them that their friend was attacked and raped on her way home from the hall in the nearby town. 'How many times have you girls been warned about going home alone, and being out so late? Your parents are always telling you, I know.'

She picks up the brown paper bag and from it takes the short skirt that the girl would have been wearing.

'This is what the silly girl was wearing. What do you girls expect to happen when you wear things like this?' She drops the skirt down onto the bag on the floor. The class are quiet, shocked by the news and the Head's condemnation of their friend (with the knowledge of the implicit condemnation of themselves). Then explanations are given:

'She was with us, it was a Beauty Competition.'

The Headmistress is shocked, 'You mean to say, you encouraged her to dress like that?' The class are caught in a dilemma, aware that they did encourage her to 'dress up' and so in a sense contributed to the attack. They react angrily to the Head's implications that she wore 'tarty' clothes:

'It was a competition!' 'Girls wear skirts like that, it's the fashion.'

'But it's not safe to go around like that, dressed in clothes like that,' replies the Head.

'Why not? It's not our fault that there are men like that about!'

A discussion follows covering the style of dress, the use of clothing and make-up in advertising. The freedom and safety of the individual and the rights of the individual. How to achieve a balance between caution and freedom if one is a woman. Are women naturally dependent upon men? Why do girls have less freedom than boys?

I wish more P.G.C.E. students could, at the end of their course, demonstrate so clearly their understanding of the nature of drama, of the use of drama in the service of education, of the sensibilities of adolescents. In a way this lesson plan epitomises what this book has been about. I have used many technical terms, particularly in my analysis of other lessons in this chapter, but such terms are not important in themselves. If the reader cares to, he or she may find within this plan examples of in context, out of context, teacher-in-role, teacher narration, dramatic playing, performance, projection, symbolisation, distancing, and game structures. But the writers use other words. It is their understanding of what they are doing that matters. There is little to be gained by attempting to learn 'Bolton's terminology'.

What is patently not in use in the 'rape' lesson plan is a 'Mantle of the Expert' frame. Had the Birmingham students wished, they could have given further distance to their project, for example by putting the pupils in role as police trainers preparing a work-shop demonstration for police recruits on how to question rape victims with sensitivity. (I can see Dorothy's mind reaching out to such distancing as 'Art Historians restoring the painting of *The Rape of the Sabine Women*'.) Unfortunately, many teachers do not appreciate the need for or know how to distance. I recently observed a lesson in a Harlem school attempting to deal with the topic of racial prejudice by *direct* enactment of an 'incident', leaving the pupils to protect themselves – which they did, by fooling around.

However, the Birmingham students find a different kind of 'frame'. The point I want to underline here is that because I have tended to use the metaphor 'frame' in respect of 'Mantle of the Expert', I may have appeared to exclude the sense in which *all drama is 'framed'*, that that is what drama is. If 'metaxis' denotes a special state of mind, a psychological state, 'frame' denotes an epistemological relationship between the knower and what is 'given'. Karl Popper (1972) is in my view wrong to suggest there is a 'third world of knowledge', the knowledge we have in our libraries. He argues that if most of the people of the world were destroyed that knowledge would remain, someday to be learnt all over again by alien visitors to our libraries. I think it is misleading to perceive this as knowledge, for knowledge only comes into existence when it is 'framed', when there is a seeker, a searcher, a learner whose perspective, however idiosyncratic, endows the printed word, the design, the map, the picture, the computer data, etc. etc. with a *focused* meaning. Learning is a process of finding a frame through which to make connections. This is another way of putting R. K. Elliott's phrase of breaking 'the domination of our ordinary habits of conceptions and perceptions'. The learner will remain, to use Phyl Herbert's phrase, but a 'passive observer of a given world' (p. 55), the 'given' remains intact and the learner's conception secure unless the focus, frame or, to go back to my own metaphor, the 'prism' is well chosen. To see drama as a 'prismatic' process is to emphasise the 'refractory' effect it has on

stereotyped understanding. In the 'rape' lesson the horror
of the incident is seen against the implicit attitudes and
values of a Beauty Contest in which the participants
gradually build a vested interest. Two apparently incompatible frames or lenses are placed one over the other so
that the perspective on each is refracted. The planning
for this lesson goes to the heart of the nature of learning.
Well-constructed drama can make connections so that
new things are understood. *It can provide its own built-in
frame or lens. It is on this that any argument for seeing drama
at the centre of the curriculum must rest.* Because I am talking
about *learning* and *understanding* some people may assume,
as Malcolm Ross (1982) tends to, that I am denying the
power of the art experience. The opposite is the case.
'She drops the skirt down onto the bag on the floor' is
written with as strong a sense of dramatic form as of
epistemology. Any playwright could give instruction for
this kind of symbolism as part of a script.

This raises two issues, one related to drama as a
performing art and the other related to the future of the
curriculum. As I suggested at the end of the last chapter,
the climate is ripe for reviving interest in Community
Theatre, to which the school as a community institution
should contribute. Many pupils in our secondary schools
will benefit from a theatre experience just as many enjoy
being in a school orchestra. As a performing art, however,
drama can make no claim to a higher status than dance
or music. They are all equally important as celebration.
A special case for drama can only be made in regard to
its potency as a model for learning that is both psychological and social.

In this sense drama can become a pivot of the curriculum, the implementation of which can be practised
through other teachers' usage of its methodology, or by
project-centred work with drama as a core and/or by
drama as a central subject integrating with other subjects
at a level of, to use R. K. Elliott's phrase, 'common
understanding'. The kind of drama created cannot be

seen as in competition with drama as a performing art for they necessarily complement each other in that they both demand 'truthfulness' and, as has been established earlier in the book, the performance *mode* has its own contribution to make towards drama for understanding.

The second issue relates to our own ability as teachers to implement structured learning through drama. The Birmingham Polytechnic P.G.C.E. students are on an exceptional course with David Davis, an exceptional course leader. Their thinking is far in advance of many drama students coming out of training. Before we put drama at the centre of the curriculum we must be sure teachers are equipped to cope with the responsibility. However, in recent years there has been a growth of sophistication particularly in our local education authority in-service courses and in the teachers' courses promoted at Certificate and Diploma level by the Drama Board and the Royal Society of Arts. In recent visits to local schools I came across drama lessons conducted by fairly inexperienced teachers which were considerably in advance of many of those analysed in detail by the Schools Council Publication (1977). There is room, I think, for cautious optimism.

We still have a lot to learn. I have recently been looking at drama in schools in New York City. I was invited to a Junior High School in Harlem that is allowed to specialise in the arts because an East Harlem Schools Inspector has discovered that the average reading age of pupils attending schools with a strong arts bias tends to be higher than the norm. We have been slow to recognise the possible side effects of the arts. As far as I know the use of drama to teach reading has only been given any serious attention by David Booth (1978). Much more research needs to be done. We have little excuse, for the idea has been mooted from the beginning of the century. It was John Dewey who in the first decade advocated the use of dramatisation to teach reading and as a way of making abstract ideas available to pupils:

187

Allow him to act out the idea and it becomes real to him.

Thus John Dewey advised us – nearly eighty years ago.

Just a word of warning to the teacher; I have made some serious claims for drama in this book. But let us not, in our attempt to understand the educational and artistic potential of the subject, forget that Caldwell Cook saw it as the 'play-way' to education. Our perspective as teachers must be a serious one, but in setting up our learning contexts or our community arts contexts, we must not forget that for our pupils and students it *is* a 'play-way'. The essential feature is its immediate appeal as a fun thing to do. If we do not allow this fun, then we are in danger of depriving our pupils of the chance to take their fun seriously.

Bibliography

ALINGTON, A. F. (1961) *Drama and Education*, Basil Blackwell

ALLEN, JOHN (1979) *Drama in Schools: its theory and practice*, Heinemann

ARGYLE, MICHAEL, FURNHAM, ADRIAN and GRAHAM, JEAN ANN (1981) *Social Situations*, Cambridge University Press

ARIETI, SILVANO (1967) *The Intrapsychic Self*, Basic Books Inc., N.Y.

ARNHEIM, RUDOLF (1954) *Art and Visual Perception*, Berkeley

ARNHEIM, RUDOLF (1970) *Visual Thinking*, University of California Press

ARTAUD, ANTONIN (1970) *The Theatre and its Double*, trans. V. Corti, Calder

AVEDON, ELLIOTT M. and SUTTON-SMITH, BRIAN (1971) *The Study of Games*, John Wiley and Sons, N.Y.

BARISH, JONAS A. (1966) 'The Antitheatrical Prejudice', in *The Critical Quarterly*, Vol. 8, No. 4, Winter.

BARISH, JONAS A. (1969) 'Exhibitionism and the antitheatrical prejudice', in *E.L.H.*, Vol. 36, No. 1, March.

BAKER, CLIVE (1977) *Theatre Games*, Eyre Methuen

BATESON, GREGORY (1973) *Steps to an Ecology of Mind*, Paladin Books

BEST, DAVID (1978) *Objectivity in Artistic Appreciation*, International Society for Education through Art

BIRMINGHAM POLYTECHNIC P.G.C.E. DRAMA COURSE STUDENTS, Year 1981/82: J. Alloway, R. Billson, K. Cameron, G. Chesney, H. Doherty, P. Franklin, E. Maguire, M. Payne, L. Rogers, S. Shewring and C. Swift (1982) 'What is Drama?', (unpublished paper).

BOAL, AUGUSTO (1981) *Théâtre de l'opprimé*, Numero 5, Ceditade: An 03

BOARD OF EDUCATION (1905) *Handbook of Suggestions for the*

Consideration of Teachers and Others concerned in the Work of Public Elementary Schools, H.M.S.O.

BOARD OF EDUCATION (1926) *Report of the Consultative Committee on the Education of the Adolescent* (The Hadow Report), H.M.S.O.

BOARD OF EDUCATION (1931) *Report of the Consultative Committee on the Primary School*, H.M.S.O.

BOAS, G. and HAYDEN, H. (eds.) (1938) *School Drama*, Methuen

BOLTON, GAVIN M. (1977) 'Psychical Distancing in Acting', in *The British Journal of Aesthetics*, Vol. 17, No. 1, Winter.

BOLTON, GAVIN (1978) 'Emotion in the dramatic process – is it an adjective or a verb?', in *National Association for Drama in Education Journal*, Vol. 3, December 1978, pp. 14–18 (Australia).

BOLTON, GAVIN (1979) *Towards a Theory of Drama in Education*, Longman

BOLTON, GAVIN M. (1982) 'Drama as Learning', in *The Development of Aesthetic Experience* by Malcolm Ross (ed.), Curriculum Issues in Arts Education, Volume 3. Pergamon Press

BOLTON, GAVIN (1983) *Bolton at the Barbican*, National Association for Teachers of Drama

BOOTH, DAVID W. (1978) An examination of the relationship between Reading and Drama in Education, (M.Ed. thesis, University of Durham)

BRANDES, DONNA and PHILLIPS, HOWARD (1979) *Gamester's Handbook*, Access Publishing

BRANDES, DONNA (1981) *The Hope St. Experience: A teacher's true story of using drama and humanistic teaching with a difficult class*, Access Publishing

BRECHT, BERTOLT (1973) *Brecht on Theatre: The Development of an Aesthetic*, trans. J. Willett, Eyre Methuen

BRITTAN, ARTHUR (1973) *Meanings and Situations*, Routledge and Kegan Paul

BRITTON, JAMES (1970) *Language and Learning*, Penguin

BROOK, PETER (1968) *The Empty Space*, Macgibbon and Kee

BRUFORD, ROSE (1958) *Teaching Mime*, Methuen

BRUNER, JEROME S. (1971) *The Relevance of Education*, George Allen and Unwin

BULLOUGH, EDWARD (1912) 'Psychical Distancing as a Factor in Art and as an Aesthetic Principle', in *British Journal of Psychology*, 5.

CALOUSTE GULBENKIAN FOUNDATION (1982) *The Arts in Schools*, Calouste Gulbenkian Foundation

CAMPBELL-FISHER, IVY G. (1950) 'Aesthetics and the Logic of Sense', in *Journal of General Psychology*, XLIII, pp. 245–73

CARROLL, JOHN (1980) *The Treatment of Dr. Lister: A Language Functions Approach to Drama in Education*, Mitchell College of Advanced Education

CEMREL INC. (eds. Smith, L. M. and Schumacher, S.) (1972) *Extended Pilot Trials of the Aesthetic Education Program: A Qualitative Description, Analysis and Evaluation*, Cemrel, August.

CHILVER, PETER (1978) *Teaching Improvised Drama*, Batsford

COGGIN, PHILIP A. (1956) *Theatre and Education*, Thames and Hudson

COLLINS, HELEN (ed.) (1982) 'Drama and Theatre: A Shared Role in Learning', in *Mask*, Volume 6, No. 4. Victoria Association for Drama in Education and Joint Standing Committee for Drama in Schools

COOK, CALDWELL H. (1966) *The Play Way*, (First published 1917, Heinemann) Portway

COURTNEY, RICHARD (1965) *Teaching Drama*, Cassell

COURTNEY, RICHARD (1968) *Play, Drama and Thought*, Cassell

COURTNEY, RICHARD (1971) 'Drama and Pedagogy', in *Stage-Canada Supplement*, Vol. 6, No. 5a.

COWAN, PHILIP A. (1978) *Piaget with Feeling*, Holt, Rinehart and Winston

COX, C. B. and DYSON, A. E. (eds.) (1971) *The Black Papers on Education*, Davis-Poynter Ltd

COX, TIM (1970) 'The Development of Drama in Education 1902–1944', (M.Ed. thesis, University of Durham)

CRAIG, GORDON (1962) *On the Art of the Theatre*, Mercury Books

CROMPTON, N. J. R. (1978) 'A critical evaluation of the aims and purposes of drama in education', (M.Phil. thesis, University of Nottingham)

DAVIS, DAVID (1976) 'What is "Depth" in Education Drama?', in *Young Drama*, October, Vol. 4, No. 3.

DAVIS, DAVID (1982) 'An examination of the relationship of theory and practice in teacher education with special reference to the initial preparation of drama teachers', (M.Ed. thesis, University of Birmingham)

DAVIS, DAVID and ROPER, WILLIAM J. (1982) 'Theory and Practice in Teacher Education', in *European Journal of Teacher Education*, Vol. 5, No. 3

DAY, CHRISTOPHER (1975) *Drama for Middle and Upper Schools*, Batsford

DAY, CHRISTOPHER (1981) 'Classroom based in-service teacher of education: the development and evaluation of a client-centred model', (Occasional Paper, University of Sussex)

DEARDEN, ROBERT FREDERICK (1976) *Problems in Primary Education*, Routledge and Kegan Paul

DEPARTMENT OF EDUCATION AND SCIENCE (1967) *Drama. Education Survey 2*, H.M.S.O.

D.E.S. REPORT (1967) *Children and Their Primary Schools* (Plowden Committee), H.M.S.O.

D.E.S. (1978) *Primary Education in England*, H.M.S.O.

DEVERALL, JOHN (1979) 'Public Medium, Private Process: Drama, child-centred education and the growth model of human development', (M.A. (Ed.) thesis, University of Durham)

DEWEY, JOHN (u.d.) *Schools of Tomorrow*, J. M. Dent and Sons

DEWEY, JOHN (1921) *The School and Society*, University of Chicago Press

DEWEY, JOHN (1934) *Art as Experience*, Capricorn Books

DIDEROT, DENIS (1957) *The Paradox of Acting*, Hill and Wang

DONALDSON, MARGARET (1978) *Children's Minds*, Fontana/Collins

DUNLOP, F. N. (1977)'Human Nature, Learning and Ideology', in *British Journal of Education Studies*, Vol. XXV, No. 3, October, pp. 239–257

EISNER, ELLIOT W. (1979) *The Educational Imagination on the Design and Evaluation of School Programs*, Collier Macmillan

ELAM, KEIR (1980) *The Semiotics of Theatre and Drama*, Methuen

ELLIOTT, R. K. (1973) 'Imagination in the Experience of Art', in *Philosophy and the Arts*, (ed.) G. Vesey, Macmillan

ELLIOTT, R. K. (1975) 'Education and Human Being', in *Philosophers Discuss Education*, (ed.) S. Brown, Proceedings of Royal Institute of Philosophy Conference 1973, Macmillan

FAULKES-JENDYK, MARGARET (1975) 'Creative Dramatics Leaders Face Objective Examination', in *Canadian Child and Youth Drama Association Bulletin 1974* and *Children's Theatre Review*

FIALA, O. and HEATHCOTE, D. (1980) 'Brechtian Elements in Dorothy Heatcote's Approach in Preparing Teachers to Use Drama', published under title, 'Preparing Teachers to Use Drama: The Caucasian Chalk Circle', in *Drama as Context* by Dorothy Heathcote, N.A.T.E.

FINES, JOHN and VERRIER, RAYMOND (1974) *The Drama of History*, New University Education

FINLAY-JOHNSON, HARRIET (u.d.) *The dramatic method of teaching*, Nisbet

FLEMING, MICHAEL (1982) 'A philosophical investigation into drama in education', (Ph.D. thesis, University of Durham)

FREUD, SIGMUND (1952) 'Beyond the Pleasure Principle', in *The Major Works of Sigmund Freud*, Chicago Press

FROEBEL, F. (1887) *The Education of Man*, Appleton, New York (Trans. into English)

FROEBEL, F. (1912) *Froebel's Chief Writings on Education*, trans. Fletcher and Welton, Edward Arnold

GILLHAM, GEOFF (1974) 'Condercum School Report' for Newcastle upon Tyne L.E.A. (unpublished)

GILLHAM, GEOFF (1979) 'What's happening when children are doing Drama in Depth?', in *Schooling and Culture*, Issue 4, Spring

GOFFMAN, ERVING (1969) *The Presentation of Self in Everyday Life*, Allen Lane, The Penguin Press

GOLDMAN, MICHAEL (1975) *The Actor's Freedom: Towards a Theory of Drama*, The Viking Press, New York

GOODE, TONY (ed.) (1982) *Heathcote at the National*, National Association for the Teaching of Drama, Kemble Press

GRIFFITHS, DAVID (1970) 'The History and Role of the Drama Adviser', (Dissertation for the University of Durham's Advanced Diploma in Drama in Education (unpublished))

GROOS, KARL (1899) *The Play of Man*, Appleton Press

HALL, G. S. (1904) *Adolescence*, Appleton-Century-Crofts

HAMILTON, D., JENKINS, D., KING, C. and PARLETT, M. (eds.) (1977) *Beyond the Numbers Game*, Macmillan

HAMLYN, DAVID WALTER (1973) 'Human Learning', in *The Philosophy of Education*, (ed.) Richard S. Peters, Oxford University Press

HAMLYN, DAVID WALTER (1978) *Experience and the Growth of Understanding*, Routledge and Kegan Paul

HANEY, C., BANKS, W. C. and ZIMBARDO, P. G. (1973) 'Inter-personal dynamics in a simulated prison', in *International Journal of Criminology and Penology*, 1, pp. 69–97

HARGREAVES, DAVID (1982) *The Challenge for the Comprehensive School*, Routledge and Kegan Paul

HARRÉ, ROM (1979) *Social Being*, Basil Blackwell

HEATHCOTE, DOROTHY (1980) *Drama as Context*, N.A.T.E.

HEATHCOTE, DOROTHY (1980) 'Material for Meaning in Drama', in *London Drama*

HEATHCOTE, DOROTHY (1982) 'Signs and Portents?', in *SCYPT JOURNAL*, No. 9, April

HERBERT, PHYL A. (1982) 'A theory of Education as presented through the Drama Process "Mantle of the Expert"', (M.Ed. dissertation, University of Newcastle upon Tyne)

HERRON, R. E. and SUTTON-SMITH, B. (1971) *Child's Play*, Wiley

HEYFRON, VICTOR (1982) 'The Aesthetic Dimension in Art Education: A Phenomenological View', in *The Development of Aesthetic Experience*, (ed.) Malcolm Ross, pp. 27–46, Pergamon Press

HIRST, PAUL H. and PETERS, RICHARD S. (1970) *The Logic of Education*, Routledge and Kegan Paul

HODGSON, JOHN and BANHAM, MARTIN (1972, 1973, 1975) *Drama in Education, Books 1, 2 and 3* , Pitman

HOLMES, EDMOND (1914) *In Defence of What Might Be*, Constable

HUIZINGA, JOHAN (1970) *A Study of the Play Element in Culture*, Temple Smith

HUNT, ALBERT (1976) *Hopes for Great Happenings*, Eyre Methuen

JACKSON, ANTHONY (1980) *Learning through Theatre*, Manchester University Press

JENNINGS, SUE (1973) *Remedial Drama: A handbook for teachers and therapists*, Pitman

JOHNSON, LIZ and O'NEILL, CECILY (1983) *Selected Writings of Dorothy Heathcote*, Hutchinson

KOLVE, V. A. (1966) *The Play Called Corpus Christi*, Edward Arnold

KOPPEL, TINA (1981) 'An Examination of Some Social Role Theories and Drama for the Adolescent', (M.A. dissertation, University of Durham)

LANGER, SUSANNE K. (1942) *Philosophy in a New Key*, Harvard University Press

LANGER, SUSANNE K. (1953) *Feeling and Form*, Routledge and Kegan Paul

LANGER, SUSANNE, K. (1975) *Mind: An Essay on Human Feeling Vol. 1.* John Hopkins Paperback

LAWRENCE, CHRIS (1982) 'Descriptive Examination of the Process of Planning a Drama Project', (Drama Diploma dissertation, University of Durham)

LEE, JOSEPH (1915) *Play in Education*, Macmillan

LINNELL, ROSEMARY (1982) *Approaching Classroom Drama*, Edward Arnold

195

MCGREGOR, LYNN (1976) 'A sociological investigation of drama teaching in three schools', (M.Phil. thesis, University of London Institute of Education)

MCGREGOR, LYNN (1976) *Developments in Drama Teaching*, Open Books

MCGREGOR, L., TATE, M. and ROBINSON, K. (1977) *Learning through Drama*, Schools Council Drama Teaching Project (10–16), Heinemann

MAGNER, BJÜORN (1972) *Improvisera octi diskutera*, Esselte Studium, Stockholm

MAROWITZ, CHARLES (1978) *The Act of Being*, Secker and Warburg

MASLOW, ABRAHAM H. (1954) *Motivation and Personality*, Harper, New York

MEAD, GEORGE HERBERT (1934) *Mind, Self and Society*, University of Chicago Press

MINISTRY OF EDUCATION (1949) *Story of a School*, Pamphlet No. 14. H.M.S.O.

MINISTRY OF EDUCATION (1949) Report of the Drama Working Party (unpublished)

MINISTRY OF EDUCATION (1963) *Half Our Future* (Newsome Committee), H.M.S.O.

MORENO, J. L. (1964) *Psychodrama*, Beacon House, New York

MOTTER, VAIL T. H. (1929) *The School Drama in England*, Longman

MURDOCH, IRIS (1970) *The Sovereignty of Good*, Routledge

NATIONAL ASSOCIATION OF TEACHERS OF DRAMA (ed. John Norman) (1981) *Report of Annual Conference 1981: Drama in Education – A Curriculum for Change*, N.A.T.D./Kemble Press

NEILL, A. S. (1964) *Summerhill*, Victor Gollancz

NORMAN, JOHN (ed.) (1981) *Drama in Education: A Curriculum for Change*, National Association for the Teaching of Drama and Kemble Press

OAKESHOTT, MICHAEL (1967) 'Learning and Teaching', in *The Concept of Education* (ed.) Richard S. Peters, Routledge and Kegan Paul

O'NEILL, CECILY, LAMBERT, ALAN, LINNELL, ROSEMARY and

196

WARR-WOOD, JANET (1976) *Drama Guidelines*, Heinemann in association with London Drama

O'NEILL, CECILY and LAMBERT, ALAN (1982) *Drama Structures*, Hutchinson

O'TOOLE, JOHN (1976) *Theatre in Education*, Unibooks, Hodder and Stoughton

PARRY, CHRISTOPHER (1972) *English through Drama*, Cambridge University Press

PEMBERTON-BILLING, ROBIN N. and CLEGG, J. DAVID (1965) *Teaching Drama*, University of London Press

PIAGET, JEAN (1967) *Play, Dreams and Imitations*, trans. C. Gattegno and F. M. Hodgson, Routledge and Kegan Paul

PIAGET, JEAN (1976) 'Symbolic Play', in *Play* by Bruner, Jerome S. et al. (eds.), pp. 555–569, Penguin

PIAGET, JEAN (1981) *Intelligence and Affectivity*, trans. T. A. Brown and C. E. Kaegi, Annual Reviews Inc., Pazlo Alto

POJMAN, LOUIS P. (1978) 'Kierkegaard's Theory of Subjectivity and Education', in *Phenomenology and Education*, Curtis, Bernard and Mays, Wolfe (ed.) Methuen

POLANYI, MICHAEL (1958) *Personal Knowledge Towards a Post-Critical Philosophy*, Routledge and Kegan Paul

POPPER, KARL (1972) *Objective Knowledge: An Evolutionary Approach*, Oxford University Press

POSTMAN, NEIL and WEINGARTNER, CHARLES (1971) *Teaching as a Subversive Activity*, Penguin

QUICK, R. H. (1902) *Essays on Educational Reformers*, Longman Green

READ, HERBERT (1943) *Education through Art*, Faber

READMAN, GEOFF (IN PREPARATION) 'The Game of Drama', (M.Ed. thesis, University of Durham)

REID, LOUIS ARNAUD (1969) *Meaning in the Arts*, George Allen and Unwin

REID, LOUIS ARNAUD (1982) 'The Concept of Aesthetic Education', in *The Development of Aesthetic Experience*, (ed.) Malcolm Ross, pp. 2–26, Pergamon Press

ROBINSON, KEN (1980) *Exploring Theatre and Education*, Heinemann

197

ROBINSON, KENNETH (1981) 'A Re-evaluation of the roles and functions of drama in secondary education with reference to a survey of curricular drama in 259 secondary schools', (Ph.D. thesis, University of London)

ROBINSON, KEN (ed.) (1982) *The Arts in Schools*, Calouste Gulbenkian Foundation, London

ROGERS, CARL (1961) *On Becoming a Person*, Constable

ROSEN, CONNIE and HAROLD (1973) *The Language of Primary School Children*, Penguin

ROSEN, HAROLD (1980) 'The Dramatic Mode', in *Coming to Know*, (ed.) Phillida, Salmon, pp. 152–169, Routledge and Kegan Paul

ROSS, MALCOLM (1978) *The Creative Arts*, Heinemann

ROSE, MALCOLM (ed.) (1982) *The Development of Aesthetic Experience*, Curriculum Series in the Arts, Volume 3, Pergamon Press

ROUSSEAU, JEAN J. (1969) *Emile*, Dent Everyman Edition

SCHATTNER, GERTRUD and COURTNEY, RICHARD (ed.) (1981) *Drama in Therapy*, Vols. 1 and 2, Drama Book Specialists, New York

SCHILLER, FRIEDRICH (1795) *On the Aesthetic Education of Man*, trans. Reginald Snell, 1965, Frederick Ungar Publishing Co., New York

SCHWEITZER, PAM (1980) *Theatre in Education*, Four Secondary Programmes, Four Junior Programmes, Five Infant Programmes, Eyre Methuen

SELF, DAVID (1978) 'The School Play as Creative Theatre', in *Young Drama*, Vol. 6, No. 1, February

SENNETT, RICHARD (1977) *The Fall of Public Man*, Cambridge University Press

SHAW, ANN M. and STEVENS, C. J. (eds.) (1979) *Drama, Theatre and the Handicapped*, The American Theatre Association

SHOTTER, JOHN (1975) *Images of Man in Psychological Research*, Methuen

SLADE, PETER (1954) *Child Drama*, University of London Press

SLADE, PETER (1968) *Experience of Spontaneity*, Longman

SMILANSKI, SARAH (1968) *The effects of sociodramatic play on disadvantaged pre-school children*, Wiley

SPOLIN, VIOLA (1963) *Improvisation for the Theatre: A handbook of teaching and directing techniques*, Northwestern University Press

STABLER, TOM (1979) *Drama in the Primary Schools*, Heinemann

STANISLAVSKI, CONSTANTIN (1937) *The Actor Prepares*, Geoffrey Bles

STENHOUSE, LAWRENCE (1981) 'Drama as a Discipline of Thinking', in *Report of Annual Conference 1981 Drama in Education: A Curriculum for Change*, Kemble Press and National Association of Teachers of Drama

STEPHENSON, NORMAN and VINCENT, DENIS (1975) *Teaching and Understanding Drama*, N.F.E.R. Publishing Co., Windsor

SULLY, JAMES (1897) *Children's Ways: Being*, Selections from the author's 'Studies of Childhood', with some additional matter, Longman

SUTHERLAND, MARGARET B. (1971) *Everyday Imagining in Education*, Routledge and Kegan Paul

TAYLOR, JOHN L and WALFORD, REX (1972) *Simulation in the Classroom*, Penguin Papers in Education

TORMEY, ALAN (1971) *The Concept of Expression*, Princeton University Press

TYNAN, KENNETH (1957) 'Theatre and Living', in *Declarations*, (ed.) Tom Maschler, pp. 108–129, Macgibbon and Kee

VERSFIELD, MARTHINUS (1972) *Persons*, Buren Publishers, Cape Town

VIOLA, W. (1942) *Child Art*, University of London Press

VYGOTSKY, L. S. (1966) 'Development of the Higher Mental Function', in *Psychological Research in the U.S.S.R*, Progress Publishers, Moscow

VYGOTSKY, LEV. S. (1933) 'Play and Its Role in the Mental Development of the Child', in *Play: Its Development and Evolution*, (eds.) Bruner *et al.* (1976) Penguin

WAGNER, BETTY JANE (1974) 'Evoking Gut-Level Drama',

in *Learning: the Magazine for Creative Teaching*, March

WAGNER, B. J. (1978) *Dorothy Heathcote: Drama as a Learning Medium*, National Education Association, Washington

WARNOCK, MARY (1976) *Imagination*, Faber and Faber

WARNOCK, MARY (1977) *Schools of Thought*, Faber and Faber

WATKINS, BRIAN (1981) *Drama and Education*, Batsford Academic and Educational

WAY, BRIAN (1967) *Development through Drama*, Longman

WEISSMAN, PHILIP (1965) *Creativity in the Theatre – a psychoanalytical study*, Basic Books, New York

WINNICOTT, D. W. (1971) *Playing and Reality*, Tavistock Publications

WITKIN, ROBERT W. (1974) *Intelligence of Feeling*, Heinemann

WITKIN, ROBERT (1978) *Art in Mind – Reflections on the Intelligence of Feeling*, International Society for Education Through Art

WOOTTON, MARGARET (ed.) (1982) *New Directions in Drama Teaching*, Heinemann

YOUNG, MICHAEL F. D. (ed.) (1971) *Knowledge and Control*, Collier-Macmillan

Index

acting 5, 7, 11, 17, 19, 22, 24, 26, 27, 38, 77, 114–129
activity method 7–9
aesthetic 16, 73, 79
Alington A. F. 67
Allen John 2, 68–70, 73
America 3, 9, 26, 42, 45, 74, 102, 103
Argyle Michael 81
Arnheim Rudolph 145
Artaud Antonin 115
Australia 1, 19

Baker, Leo 62, 63
Barish, Jonah 76, 116
Barker, Clive 74
Bateson, Gregory 80
Bennett, Stuart 43
Berman, Ed 74, 110
Berry, Cicily 65
Boas, G 4
Bolton, Gavin 56, 114, 115, 140
Brandes, Donna 74
Brecht, Bertolt 115, 142
Brittan, Arthur 122
Birmingham Polytechnic P.G.C.E. Course 180–184, 187
Booth, David 187
British Drama League 19
Brook, Peter 115, 168
Bruford, Rose 50
Bullough, Edward 115
Byron, Ken 75

Campbell-Fisher, Ivy 115

Canada 1, 8
Carroll, John 133
Cemrel Inc. 118
Chapman, Roger 43
child-centredness 4–7, 9, 14, 18, 20, 23, 27, 30, 35, 44, 47
children's theatre 43
Chilver, Peter 16
Clegg, David 44
Cobby, Maisie 2
Coggin, Philip 2
Cook, Caldwell 14–17, 20, 22, 25, 82, 165, 188
community theatre 61–67, 161–164, 186
context 156–160, 165–179
Courtney, Richard 8, 14, 31, 57
Cox Tim 2, 17, 18, 23, 28, 30
Craig, Gordon 115
Crompton, John 58

Davis, David 72, 129, 187
Day, Chris 16, 51
Dearden, R. F. 80
Deverall, John 2, 44, 46
Dewey, John 49, 187, 188
Diderot, Denis 115, 117
drama as art 2, 16, 24, 29, 47, 75, 140–164, 186
Drama Board 19, 62, 63

dramatic playing
  mode 27, 31, 32
  (definition), 33–38, 41, 100–103, 113–139
Dunlop, F. 155

Elliott, R. K. 141, 143, 144, 149, 150, 154, 185, 186
emotion 105–139
Evernden, Stan 44
exercise 31, 47, 48, 49
  (definition), 59, 113

Faulkes-Jendyk, Margaret 58, 169
Fiala, Oliver 142
Fines, John 16
Finlay-Johnston, Harriet 11–13, 15, 17, 20, 22, 34, 53, 152, 165
Fleming, Michael 148, 151, 155
focus 155–163
Fogerty, Elsie 18
Foster, Ruth 67
frame 56
Freud, Sigmund 8
Froebel, F. 4, 28

game 30, 39, 74, 76–82, 161
Garrick, David 117
Gill, Jim 67
Gillham, Geoff 43, 107, 108, 157, 159
Gilpin, Joan 15
Goffman, Erving 81, 124, 168

Goldman, Michael 121
Goode, Tony 54
Griffiths, David 61, 62, 69
Groos, Karl 8
Gulbenkian, Caloustie Report 64, 73, 161

Hadow Report 17, 23
Haggerty, Joan 11
Hall, G. S. 8
Hamlyn, D. W. 155
Hargreaves, David 46, 60, 64
Harré, Rom 81, 112, 116
Heathcote, Dorothy 2, 12, 14, 15, 42–59, 64, 72, 74, 94, 95, 110, 121–133, 142, 158, 165–180
Hedley, Philip 68
Herbert, Phyl 173–180, 185
Hirst, Paul 149
Hodson, Geoffery 72
Hodgson, John 2, 74, 75
Holmes, Edward 7, 9
Huizinga, Johan 78, 79, 109
Hunt, Albert 26
Husbands, Peter 63

Jackson, Tony 43
James, Peter 68
Jenner, Caryl 43
Jennings, Sue 74
Johnson, Liz 58
Johnstone, Keith 68

King, Collette 68
knowledge 3–5, 8, 10, 12, 20, 50, 52, 55, 57, 59, 73, 143–164
Kolve, V. A. 77, 78

Laban, Rudolf 67, 68
Lambert, Alan 82, 93, 95, 98, 171, 172

Langer, Susanne 115, 147
language 10
Lawrence, Chris 133, 168
learning 8, 9, 72, 73, 142, 148–164, 185, 186
Lee, Jenny 69
Lee, Joseph 8, 28–31

Mackenzie, Frances 62
Magner, Bjorn 75
mantle of the expert 57, 173–180
Marowitz, Charles 118–121
Maslow, Abraham 45
Mcgregor, Lynn 16, 70
Mead, George Herbert 100
Moreno, J, L, 110
Moreton, David 64
Moss Ray 70
Motter, Vail 4
Murdoch, Iris 46, 154

Neill, A. S. 4
New Education Movement 7, 8, 20
Newsom Report 4
Newton, Robert 62
Norman, John 141, 148

O'Neill, Cecily 16, 58, 82, 93, 95, 171, 172
O'Toole, John 43

Pammeter, David 43
Parry, Christopher 14, 16
Pemberton-Billing, Robin 44
performing mode 25, 28, 32 (definition), 37–41, 102, 104, 113–139
Peters, R. S. 80, 149
Piaget, Jean 39, 81
Plaskow, Maurice 70

play 7, 14, 16, 28, 31, 34, 39, 79–81, 170–171
Plowden Report 4, 10, 44
Polanyi, Michael 103, 155, 156
Popper, Karl 185
Price, Maureen 72
protection 128–139

Quick, R. H. 8

Read, Herbert 16
Readman, Geoff 76, 92
Reid, Louis Arnaud 79, 143, 147
Robinson, Ken 2, 4, 18, 20, 40, 70, 74, 116, 140
Robson, Mary 69
Rogers, Carl 45
role function 101, 104, 105, 119, 123, 140, 143, 151
Rosen, Connie and Harold 10, 53
Ross, Malcolm 75, 101, 140, 152, 153, 167, 186

Schweitzer, Pam 43
Self, David 161
self-expression 5–7, 11, 14, 20, 22, 34, 40, 46, 94, 120–22
Sennett, Richard 46, 117
Slade, Peter 2, 6, 8, 11, 21–24, 28–44, 52, 55, 60–64, 70, 101, 110, 131, 142, 158, 165–71
Smilanski, Sarah 81
speech-training 17–20, 24–26, 40, 44
spiritual 16, 21, 23, 152, 153
Spolin, Viola 74
Stabler, Tom 53, 70
Stanislavski,